EARL NIGHTINGALE'S

THE STRANGEST SECRET:

70 YEARS LATER

By Vic Johnson

EARL NIGHTINGALE'S
THE STRANGEST SECRET:
70 YEARS LATER

By Vic Johnson

****

Published by:
Sylvia's Foundation, Inc.
PO Box 1220
Melrose, FL 32666 USA

Media@sylvias-love.org

****

© Copyright 2025 Sylvia's Foundation, Inc. All rights reserved. Without limiting the rights under copyright reserved above, no part of this publication may be reproduced, stored in or introduced into a retrieval system, or transmitted, in any form, or by any means (electronic, mechanical, photocopying, recording, or otherwise) without the prior written permission of both the copyright owner and the above publisher of this book.

ISBN-13: 978-1-937918-06-4

Printed in the United States of America.

TABLE OF CONTENTS

Preface 1

Introduction: Earl Nightingale - The Dean of
Personal Development 5

Early Life: A Hunger for Knowledge 6

A Turning Point in World War II 6

The Birth of The Strangest Secret 7

The Nightingale-Conant Corporation 10

Philosophies and Core Beliefs 10

Legacy and Impact 11

The Timeless Voice of Wisdom 12

The Legacy Lives On 13

Chapter 1: We Become What We Think About 15

The Mind as a Garden 16

The Science of Thought 17

Real-World Examples 18

How This Law Affects Your Daily Life 22

Action Steps to Reprogram Your Thinking 23

The Unbreakable Truth 25

Chapter 2: The Fear of Conformity.....................26
Why Do People Conform? 27
The Cost of Following the Crowd 30
Real-World Examples of Thinking Differently.........31
The Rise of Independent Careers 33
How to Break Free from Conformity 34
Key Thought to Remember 38
Action Steps – Break Free from the Herd 39
Final Word 39

Chapter 3: The Power of Goals 40
The Fundamental Truth About Goal-Setting 40
Clarity is Power..41
The SMART Goal Framework 42
Real-World Examples of Goals in Action..................43
The Science of Writing Down Goals – The John Goddard Story 44
Dr. Gail Matthews' Research – The Power of Writing Goals 45
The Bucket List Effect 45
Success Leaves Clues...46

The Think on Paper Method 46

Overcoming Obstacles – The Reality of Goal-Setting 47

Action Steps – Setting and Achieving Your Goal 49

The Final Word 49

Chapter 4: Success as the Progressive Realization of a Worthy Ideal 50

The Importance of Defining Success for Yourself ... 51

Success is a Journey, Not a Destination 52

Real-World Examples of Success as a Journey 53

The Role of Failure in Success 55

What These Stories Teach Us 59

Action Steps: Turning Failure into Fuel for Success 59

How to Define and Pursue Your Worthy Ideal 60

Action Steps – Living a Successful Life 61

Final Thought 62

Chapter 5: The Science of Habits 63

Why Habits Matter More Than Motivation 64

How Habits Are Formed: The Habit Loop 65

Real-World Examples of Habits Shaping Success 67

The Common Theme: Habits Build Success 70
How to Build Life-Changing Habits 71
The Habit Formula for Success 73
Missed a Day? FIDO – Forget It, Drive On 73
Action Steps: Take Control of Your Habits Today 75
Final Thought 75

Chapter 6: The Role of Service 76
Why Service Determines Success 77
The Mindset of Service vs. Selfishness 78
Real-World Examples of Service Leading to Success 79
The Service Formula for Success 82
How to Make Service a Habit 83
Final Thought: Success Follows Service 86

Chapter 7: Gratitude Unleashed – The Hidden Power That Changes Everything 87
Why Gratitude is the Key to Unlocking a Better Life 88
Real-World Examples of Gratitude in Action 89
Gratitude Connects You With Your Creator 92

What the World's Major Faiths Teach About Gratitude.................93

The Universal Power of Gratitude.................97

The Ultimate Power of Gratitude: A Strong Finish.................97

How to Make Gratitude a Daily Habit.................99

How to Deepen Your Spiritual Connection Through Gratitude.................101

Action Steps: Unleash the Power of Gratitude.................103

Final Thought: Gratitude is the Force That Unlocks Everything.................103

Chapter 8: Action and Persistence – The Twin Forces of Success.................105

Why Most People Fail: The Curse of Inaction and Weak Persistence.................106

Persistence: The True Test of Success.................107

Real-World Examples of Action and Persistence in Motion.................108

The Two Rules of Persistence: What to Do When You Want to Quit.................113

Action Steps: How to Turn Relentless Action into a Habit.................114

Final Thought: The World Belongs to the Doers..115

Chapter 9: The New Gold Mine – Creativity and Innovation 116

Why Most People Never Innovate 117

The Power of Thinking Differently 120

How to Train Yourself to Think Like an Innovator 125

Action Steps: How to Unlock Your Creative Power 126

Final Thought: The Future Belongs to the Creators 127

Chapter 10: The 30-Day Experiment – Reinventing Yourself One Month at a Time 128

The Power of the 30-Day Challenge – A Proven Path to Transformation 128

Why 30 Days? The Science Behind Short-Term Transformation 130

The Verdict: 30 Days is the Fast Track to Transformation 135

The Rules of the 30-Day Experiment 135

Real-World Examples of 30-Day Transformations 136

How to Design Your Own 30-Day Experiment 137

What Happens After 30 Days? 139

Action Steps: Start Your 30-Day Experiment Today.. 140
Final Thought: The Power of One Month............... 140

Chapter 11: Wealth and the Law of Mutual Exchange.. 142
Why Most People Struggle Financially 143
The Wealth Formula: How to Create Massive Value.. 144
The Bottom Line: Value First, Money Follows....... 149
Real-World Examples of Wealth Creation 149
The Takeaway: Wealth Comes from Vision, Action, and Scale 153
Action Steps: How to Attract Wealth Starting Today.. 154
Final Thought: Money is a Reflection of Value...... 155

Chapter 12: A Life Worth Living................................. 156
What Does It Mean to Live a Life Worth Living? . 157
The Four Pillars of a Life Worth Living.................... 158
Final Thought: Live with Intention 163

About The Author 166
Other Books by Vic Johnson 168

PREFACE

The first time I heard Earl Nightingale's distinctive, resonant voice, I was a young man in my twenties, hungry for direction. Even now, more than 50 years later, his wisdom still feels fresh—just as thrilling and relevant as it did the first time I encountered it.

His words gave me something I desperately needed back then: hope. I was a college dropout with no remarkable skills, no clear path to success—just a vague notion that life could be more than what I was living. Earl, along with mentors like Denis Waitley, planted a seed in me—a belief that I could one day stand where they stood, teaching people how to dream bigger, live with purpose, and achieve more than they ever thought possible. What I never imagined in those early days was just how close I would eventually come to the man himself.

One of my greatest mentors, Bob Proctor, had once worked for Earl as a Vice President at Nightingale-

Conant. In fact, Bob was part of the company when I first discovered Earl's teachings through a direct mail sales letter. Years later, my path led me to a nearly two-decade-long mentorship with Bob, a relationship that profoundly shaped my life. We spent countless hours together, and Earl's name surfaced often in conversation—always spoken with deep admiration and reverence. Bob valued every lesson he had learned from Earl, and as his mentee, I inherited the wisdom of both men.

Another unexpected link to the "Dean of Personal Development" came through his second wife, Diana. Over the years, I collaborated with her on several projects to bring Earl's work to a wider audience. I even had the privilege of visiting her home in Arizona, where I spent an unforgettable morning sifting through relics of Earl's extraordinary career—artifacts of a man whose impact has spanned generations.

When I first set out to revisit *The Strangest Secret* seventy years later, I wasn't sure what I would find. The world today barely resembles the one Earl spoke to in the 1950s. Back then, certain values—discipline, persistence, self-reliance—were the foundation of personal success. Now, we live in an era of instant gratification, where patience and hard work can sometimes feel outdated, even mocked.

Yet, as I dug deeper, I discovered something profound: Earl's principles remain just as powerful as ever. Why? Because they are timeless—rooted not in passing trends, but in the fundamental truths of human nature. Some modern authors (myself included) may dress them up in new packaging, adding fresh metaphors or branding to make them feel "new." But the essence remains unchanged. "As a man thinketh in his heart, so is he." That wisdom, first recorded in Proverbs, is found in the original self-improvement book—the Bible—and existed long before that.

What *has* changed, however, are the tools we now have at our disposal. In 1956, listening to *The Strangest Secret* meant gathering around a phonograph. A few ambitious individuals even installed record players in their cars—until, of course, they hit a pothole and sent the needle skipping. Today, you can stream Earl's message in the middle of the Mojave Desert, in a Manhattan taxi, or as you drift off to sleep at night. The medium has evolved, but the message remains untouched.

And that brings us to this book.

Seventy years later, *The Strangest Secret* still holds the power to transform lives. But what does it mean for *you*, here and now? How can these ideas—originally recorded in a world so different from ours—help you navigate *today's* challenges?

Let's begin.

INTRODUCTION:
EARL NIGHTINGALE - THE DEAN OF PERSONAL DEVELOPMENT

Earl Nightingale, often referred to as the "Dean of Personal Development," was a legendary figure in the self-improvement industry. Known for his powerful voice, profound insights, and groundbreaking ideas, Nightingale inspired millions through his timeless messages. His 1956 recording, *The Strangest Secret*, was the first spoken-word recording to achieve Gold Record status, cementing his place as a pioneer in the field of motivational speaking and personal development. But the story of Earl Nightingale is much more than a single achievement—it's a tale of perseverance, curiosity, and an unwavering belief in the power of the human mind.

Early Life: A Hunger for Knowledge

Earl Nightingale was born on March 12, 1921, in Long Beach, California. Growing up during the Great Depression, his family faced significant financial hardship. When his father abandoned the family, leaving Earl, his two brothers, and their mother to fend for themselves, young Earl was thrust into a world of uncertainty. Despite the challenges, Nightingale displayed an insatiable hunger for knowledge from a young age.

As a boy, he frequently visited the local library, seeking answers to the big questions that intrigued him. Chief among them was: "Why do some people succeed while others fail?" This question would later become the cornerstone of his life's work. Inspired by the writings of great philosophers and thinkers like Napoleon Hill, Ralph Waldo Emerson, and Marcus Aurelius, Nightingale began to develop a fascination with the principles of success and personal achievement.

A Turning Point in World War II

At the age of 17, Nightingale joined the United States Marine Corps. During World War II, he served aboard the USS Arizona, a battleship stationed at

Pearl Harbor. On December 7, 1941, during the infamous Japanese attack, Nightingale was one of only a handful of survivors from the USS Arizona's crew. The tragedy left a profound impact on him, further deepening his resolve to understand life's purpose and how to live it meaningfully.

After the war, Nightingale continued his pursuit of knowledge, drawing from his harrowing experiences and the resilience it took to survive and rebuild. His time in the Marines taught him discipline, focus, and the importance of mental fortitude—qualities that would define his later work.

The Birth of *The Strangest Secret*

Sometimes, the most powerful ideas are born in the simplest moments.

Earl Nightingale didn't set out to create history that morning in 1955. He wasn't thinking about bestsellers or Gold Records. He was simply responding to a request—one that would change his life and the world of personal development forever.

At the time, Nightingale was a successful radio personality and the owner of a small life insurance agency in Chicago. His passion wasn't just selling policies—it was unlocking the potential in people. He studied the great thinkers, from Marcus Aurelius to Napoleon Hill, and passed their wisdom along to his sales team in weekly motivational talks.

One day, as he prepared to leave for an extended fishing trip, his sales manager approached him with a simple request:

> **"Earl, could you leave behind a recorded message for the team? Something to keep them inspired while you're gone?"**

It seemed like a small favor, but what came next would reshape the landscape of success literature.

Nightingale woke up in the middle of the night and went to his typewriter. In a matter of hours, he distilled everything he had learned about success into a single, undeniable truth:

> **"We become what we think about."**

That was it. That was *the strangest secret.* The idea had been hidden in plain sight, woven into history, philosophy, religion, and self-improvement. Yet, few truly grasped its power.

With the concept clear in his mind, Nightingale recorded his message in one take—just him, his voice, and a microphone. No fancy production, no second drafts. He handed the recording to his sales manager and set off on his trip, giving it little further thought.

What happened next was something even Nightingale couldn't have predicted.

The sales team listened to the recording. Then, they listened again. And again. The message resonated so deeply that they began sharing it with family, friends, and colleagues.

Word spread like wildfire. People outside the company started requesting copies. The demand grew so overwhelming that the agency had to start charging for the recordings just to keep up with distribution.

Soon, *The Strangest Secret* was no longer just an internal sales tool—it was a movement.

Within months, the recording had reached **over a million people.** In an era where audio success was reserved for music, *The Strangest Secret* shattered expectations by becoming **the first spoken-word recording to receive a Gold Record certification.**

This wasn't a carefully marketed product. **It was a truth so powerful that it spread on its own.** The recording wasn't polished, edited, or rehearsed. It was pure, direct, and authentic—and that's what made it unstoppable.

The Nightingale-Conant Corporation

Encouraged by the overwhelming response to *The Strangest Secret*, Nightingale partnered with Lloyd Conant, a visionary businessman with a shared passion for personal development. Together, they founded the Nightingale-Conant Corporation, which became the leading producer of audio programs on personal development, business, and motivation.

Under Nightingale's leadership, the company produced groundbreaking works by thought leaders like Zig Ziglar, Jim Rohn, Denis Waitley, and Tony Robbins. Nightingale's own programs, such as *Lead the Field*, became staples in the personal development world. Through Nightingale-Conant, he helped shape the industry, making life-changing ideas accessible to millions.

Philosophies and Core Beliefs

Earl Nightingale's teachings were rooted in the timeless wisdom of thinkers from various disciplines, but his ability to make these ideas relatable and actionable set him apart. He believed that success was not a matter of luck or circumstance but a predictable result of consistent thought and effort. Some of his core principles included:

- **The Power of Thought**: Nightingale's famous axiom, "We become what we think about," underscores the idea that thoughts are the foundation of all success or failure.
- **Definiteness of Purpose**: He stressed the importance of having clear, specific goals and working toward them daily.
- **Self-Discipline**: Success, he believed, requires discipline and the ability to stay focused on long-term objectives despite short-term challenges.
- **Personal Responsibility**: Nightingale taught that each person has the power to shape their own destiny through their choices and actions.

Through his programs, books, and lectures, Nightingale inspired his audience to harness these principles to achieve success in all areas of life.

Legacy and Impact

Earl Nightingale's influence extended far beyond his lifetime. His teachings became a cornerstone of the personal development movement, and his voice—a deep, authoritative tone that exuded wisdom and clarity—remains iconic to this day.

Nightingale authored several books, including *This Is Earl Nightingale*, a collection of his essays and radio broadcasts, and *The Essence of Success*. His audio programs, most notably *The Strangest Secret* and *Lead the Field*, continue to be bestsellers in the self-help genre.

Earl Nightingale passed away on March 25, 1989, but his ideas endure, touching new generations of listeners and readers. His work laid the foundation for countless self-help authors and motivational speakers who followed, making him one of the most significant figures in personal development history.

The Timeless Voice of Wisdom

Earl Nightingale's life was a testament to the principles he taught. From his humble beginnings during the Great Depression to surviving the attack on Pearl Harbor and becoming a beacon of inspiration for millions, Nightingale lived a life of purpose, curiosity, and unwavering dedication to helping others unlock their potential.

His teachings remain as relevant today as they were when he first recorded *The Strangest Secret*. In a world filled with distractions and uncertainty, Nightingale's message serves as a reminder of the profound power of our thoughts and the limitless potential within each of us. Through his words, Earl Nightingale continues to inspire individuals to think bigger, act bolder, and live more meaningful lives.

The Legacy Lives On

Seventy years after *The Strangest Secret* was first recorded, its message remains as powerful as ever. The world has changed—technology has advanced, industries have evolved, and the pace of life has accelerated—but the fundamental truth that Earl Nightingale shared endures: *We become what we think about.*

In an era flooded with distractions, negativity, and information overload, Nightingale's wisdom is more crucial than ever. His voice still calls out, urging us to take control of our thoughts, set clear goals, and cultivate a mindset of success. He reminds us that true achievement isn't reserved for the lucky few— it's available to anyone willing to think intentionally, act purposefully, and persist relentlessly.

His legacy is not just in the words he spoke, but in the lives he changed. Entrepreneurs, artists, executives, and everyday individuals continue to apply his principles to create extraordinary results. His teachings have influenced generations of thought leaders, proving that personal development is not a trend but a timeless foundation for success.

So now, the question is no longer about whether *The Strangest Secret* is relevant today—it clearly is. The question is: *What will you do with it?*

You hold the same key that Nightingale discovered all those years ago. You have the power to shape your destiny through your thoughts, decisions, and actions. The principles he shared are not just theories—they are a roadmap. But only if you apply them.

Seventy years later, the secret is no longer strange—it's proven. And it is yours to use.

The time to begin is now.

CHAPTER 1:
WE BECOME WHAT WE THINK ABOUT

Core Principle: *You are the sum total of your thoughts. What you dwell upon, you become.*

Earl Nightingale revealed one of life's greatest secrets: **we become what we think about.** It is a truth as old as civilization itself, yet so few ever grasp its significance. The mind is like fertile soil—whatever you plant in it, good or bad, will take root and grow. If you consistently think about success, growth, and opportunity, they will manifest in your life. But if your mind is filled with doubt, fear, and failure, that, too, will shape your destiny.

This is not wishful thinking; it is a fundamental law of human nature. Our thoughts influence our beliefs, our beliefs dictate our actions, and our actions determine our results. Understand this, and you will hold the key to transforming your life.

The Mind as a Garden

Imagine your mind as a plot of land. It does not care what you plant—flowers or weeds, prosperity or failure. It will return what is sown with equal measure. A person who consistently nurtures thoughts of progress, confidence, and determination will reap a harvest of success. Conversely, a person who allows negative, self-defeating thoughts to take root will find their life filled with limitation and struggle.

This is why two people can face the same circumstances and produce entirely different outcomes. One sees opportunity, the other sees failure. One expects prosperity, the other braces for disaster. **Their thoughts make the difference.**

A study conducted by Dr. Martin Seligman at the University of Pennsylvania found that optimistic individuals achieve significantly greater success in life than their pessimistic counterparts. Why? Because optimism leads to action. Pessimism leads to hesitation. The thoughts you entertain will dictate your behavior and, ultimately, your future.

This principle is echoed across history. The great Roman Emperor Marcus Aurelius wrote, "A man's life is what his thoughts make of it." Ralph Waldo Emerson famously stated, "A man is what he thinks about all day long." The message has been clear for centuries, yet so few take control of their thinking.

The Science of Thought

Modern science has now confirmed what Nightingale understood decades ago:

- **Neuroplasticity**: The brain physically rewires itself based on repeated thought patterns. If you dwell on success, your mind strengthens the pathways that lead you toward it. If you focus on limitations, those pathways also become reinforced.
- **The Reticular Activating System (RAS)**: This neurological system acts as a filter, directing your attention toward what you deem important. If you constantly think about opportunities, your brain will begin to notice them everywhere. If you focus on obstacles, that is all you will see.
- **Cognitive Conditioning**: The subconscious mind does not differentiate between reality

and a vividly imagined thought. This is why visualization is so powerful—your brain begins acting as if success is already happening.
- **The Placebo Effect**: Studies show that people who believe they are receiving treatment often experience actual physiological benefits, even when given a sugar pill. This underscores the immense power of belief and thought in shaping our experiences.

Real-World Examples

- **Bob Proctor's** journey began in humble, uncertain circumstances. As a young man, he had no formal education, no direction, and was struggling financially, working dead-end jobs with no clear future. Then he discovered *Think and Grow Rich* by Napoleon Hill and later became a devoted student of Earl Nightingale's teachings. Proctor absorbed the principle that thoughts shape reality, realizing that successful people visualize their future before they achieve it. He transformed his life by obsessively applying visualization and goal-setting, going from earning a few thousand dollars a year to millions. His success became a lifelong mission—teaching others how focused thinking could create real-world results.

- As a child, **Michael Phelps** was diagnosed with ADHD, struggling to focus in school. His father, whom he idolized, left the family when Phelps was just nine, a devastating blow that fueled deep-seated feelings of abandonment and anger. Rather than let these emotions define him, Phelps channeled his energy into swimming, using visualization as a mental anchor. His coach, Bob Bowman, taught him to mentally rehearse each race, stroke by stroke, before ever touching the water. This habit became his edge, allowing him to perform flawlessly under pressure. The result? 23 Olympic gold medals, proving the power of mental preparation and belief.
- **Henry Ford's** bankruptcies are essential to his story. Before founding the Ford Motor Company, he failed twice, with his first two automobile ventures going bankrupt. Investors lost faith, and many labeled him a dreamer without business sense. But Ford never abandoned his belief that the automobile should be accessible to the average American. Rather than accept failure, he refined his

vision, introduced the assembly line to cut costs, and proved the skeptics wrong. His persistence revolutionized industry, making cars affordable for the masses and cementing his legacy as the man who redefined transportation through sheer belief and innovation.

- **Andrew Carnegie** was born into poverty in Scotland, immigrating to the United States as a child. At 13 years old, he worked 12-hour shifts in a cotton factory, earning $1.20 a week. But Carnegie never saw himself as a poor laborer—he believed in success before he had it. He studied business, invested wisely, and seized every opportunity, eventually revolutionizing the steel industry by applying compound growth principles to production. His fortune became one of the largest in history, but his mindset shaped it first. Later, he gave away 90% of his wealth, proving that a vision of success leads to lasting impact.
- **Jim Carrey** grew up in a struggling, working-class family, even living out of a van at one point. As a teenager, he dreamed of becoming a world-class comedian and actor, but no one was handing him opportunities. Instead of accepting his circumstances, Carrey wrote

himself a check for $10 million for "acting services rendered" and dated it five years in the future. Every day, he carried it in his wallet, visualizing himself cashing it. He took relentless action—performing in clubs, facing rejection, refining his craft. In 1994, just before the date on his check, he landed *Dumb and Dumber*—for $10 million.

- **Elon Musk** risked everything to pursue his vision of revolutionizing space travel and sustainable energy. After selling PayPal, he poured his entire fortune into Tesla and SpaceX—only to watch both companies teeter on the edge of collapse. By 2008, Tesla was struggling with production delays, and SpaceX had three consecutive rocket failures, leaving Musk nearly bankrupt. Critics called him delusional. But he refused to waver, visualizing a future where humanity explored Mars and drove electric cars. His persistence paid off—SpaceX's fourth launch succeeded, Tesla secured funding, and both companies reshaped their industries. His belief made the impossible, inevitable.

How This Law Affects Your Daily Life

Take a moment to reflect: What dominates your thoughts?

When you wake up in the morning, is your first instinct to dwell on problems, stress, and limitations? Or do you approach the day with a sense of possibility and expectation? Your answer reveals the trajectory of your life.

A person who constantly thinks about debt and struggle will always seem to find more bills, more unexpected expenses, more roadblocks. Why? Because their mind is trained to notice lack (Remember the RAS example above?). They reinforce a scarcity mindset every single day. When opportunities arise, they dismiss them as too risky or impossible. They act out of fear, hesitate on decisions, and unintentionally invite more struggle.

Now consider the opposite. A person who focuses on solutions, growth, and wealth-building will begin to notice new ways to create income, expand skills, and build valuable relationships. Their mind is attuned to opportunity. They are proactive instead of reactive. Rather than dwell on problems, they ask: What's the next step? They act, adjust, and persist.

This isn't magic—it's focus. What you think about shapes what you look for, and what you look for shapes what you find. Your thoughts lead to actions. Those actions, repeated, become habits. And your habits define your future. Change your thinking, and you change everything.

Action Steps to Reprogram Your Thinking

1. **Monitor Your Thoughts Daily**
   - Carry a small notebook and jot down recurring thoughts.
   - At the end of the day, categorize them: Are they empowering or limiting?

2. **Eliminate Negative Self-Talk**
   - Replace statements like "I can't" with "How can I?"
   - Challenge doubts with facts—remind yourself of past successes.

3. **Create a Vision Board**
   - Find images that represent your goals and place them where you see them daily.
   - Reinforce these images with powerful affirmations.

4. **Surround Yourself with Positive Influence**
    - Read books that inspire growth.
    - Avoid negative news and toxic conversations.
    - Spend time with people who uplift and challenge you.

5. **Visualize Success Every Morning**
    - Spend five minutes picturing yourself achieving your goals.
    - Feel the emotions associated with your success—this strengthens neural pathways.

6. **Commit to the 30-Day Challenge**
    - Nightingale issued a challenge in "The Strangest Secret"—a 30-day experiment where participants would deliberately control their thoughts and focus only on what they wanted to achieve. Those who accepted the challenge experienced extraordinary transformations. You can do the same.

For the next 30 days, consciously direct your thoughts toward growth, abundance, and achievement. Guard your mind as you would a valuable treasure. Refuse to let fear or doubt take residence. Focus only on what you desire, and watch as your world begins to change before your eyes.

The Unbreakable Truth

Success is not reserved for the lucky or the privileged. It is available to anyone who masters their thinking. You already possess the greatest tool for transformation—your mind. Use it wisely, and you will forge a future beyond your wildest dreams.

This is **The Strangest Secret**. And now, it belongs to you.

Grab Your Free Workbook and Start Your 30-Day Transformation Today

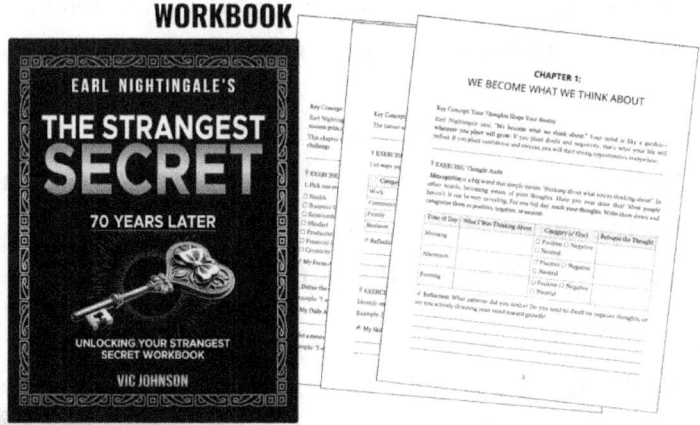

BonusWorkbook.com

SCAN ME

CHAPTER 2:

THE FEAR OF CONFORMITY

Core Principle: *Most people fail because they follow the crowd instead of thinking for themselves.*

Success is not for the average person—because the average person does what everyone else does. They think the way they're told to think. They follow the crowd. And they get the same results as everyone else.

Earl Nightingale made one thing clear: if you want what the majority has, do what the majority does. But if you want success, independence, and financial freedom, you must think differently. You must reject the natural pull toward conformity—the pull that keeps people in mediocrity, trapped by routines and fears they never stop to question.

Most people drift through life without a plan, taking whatever job is offered, following whatever path seems safest. They never stop to ask: *Do I really want this? Am I following my own path, or someone else's?* That's why **only 5% of people achieve real success.**

The difference? The successful minority think for themselves. They decide what they want, and they refuse to conform to fear-based thinking, societal pressure, and the expectations of others.

Why Do People Conform?

Conformity is the invisible thread stitching society together—and sometimes strangling individuality in the process. It's why we nod along in meetings we don't understand, wear jeans when everyone else does, or stay silent when we disagree. But why do we bend so easily to the crowd? The answer isn't just social pressure—it's etched into our DNA, a relic of survival that's been hijacked by modern life. From ancient tribes to TikTok trends, conformity is both a superpower and a shackle, driven by biology, psychology, and the human need to belong.

At its core, conformity is an evolutionary hangover. Our ancestors didn't survive the savannah by going rogue—lone wolves got eaten; group-thinkers thrived. Sticking to the tribe meant shared food, protection from saber-toothed cats, and a better shot at passing on genes. Neuroscientist Matthew Lieberman argues in *Social: Why Our Brains Are Wired to Connect* that our brains evolved to prioritize social cohesion over solo brilliance. The amygdala, our fear-alarm system, lights up when we risk ostracism—say, by challenging the chief's bad idea. Meanwhile, the prefrontal cortex, which handles reasoning, often bows to the dopamine hit of group approval. Conformity, then, isn't just learned; it's baked into our neural circuitry, a genetic nudge to play nice and stay alive.

This DNA-driven instinct shows up early. Studies like those from the Max Planck Institute reveal kids as young as two mimic peers to fit in—think toddlers copying each other's block-stacking, even when it's nonsense. By adolescence, it's turbocharged: a 2011 Neuron study found teens' reward centers flare brighter when their choices match the group's, thanks to a still-maturing brain craving acceptance. Evolutionary biologists like Robert Trivers call this "reciprocal altruism"—we conform to build trust, ensuring others have our back later. Our genes whisper: "Blend in, or get left behind."

But it's not all biology—psychology amplifies the signal. Solomon Asch's 1950s line-length experiments proved how we'll doubt our own eyes if everyone else picks the wrong answer. In his tests, 75% of people conformed at least once, choosing a blatantly incorrect line to match the group, driven by what psychologists call "normative influence"—the urge to be liked. Then there's "informational influence," where we assume the crowd knows better, especially under uncertainty. Ever followed a stranger's confident stride in a new city, only to end up lost? That's your DNA's old tribal trust kicking in, assuming collective wisdom trumps your gut.

Modern life twists this further. Social media, with its likes and retweets, is a conformity engine—our brains treat digital approval like a hunter-gatherer's nod of respect. A 2023 UCLA study found Instagram users tweak posts to match trending aesthetics, even when it feels inauthentic, echoing our ancestors' need to signal loyalty. Capitalism plays too: brands thrive on us buying the same Nikes or iPhones, exploiting what anthropologist Robin Dunbar calls our "150-person tribal limit"—we conform to imaginary clans beyond our actual circles. Our DNA didn't evolve for hashtags, but it still pulls us to the herd.

Yet conformity's grip isn't absolute—our genes also code for rebellion. The same survival drive that favors groups rewards outliers who innovate: the hunter who tries a new trap, the storyteller who spins a wilder tale. Dopamine spikes not just for fitting in but for standing out when it works—think of the thrill when a risky idea pays off. A 2020 *Nature* study on genetic markers like DRD4, linked to risk-taking, suggests some of us are wired to resist the crowd more than others. Conformity's in our DNA, but so is the itch to break free—it's a tug-of-war between safety and progress.

So why do we conform? It's a cocktail of evolutionary survival, brain chemistry, and social cues, stirred by a world that punishes misfits but craves their breakthroughs. Our DNA says "stick together," a holdover from when dissent meant death. Today, it's less about lions and more about likes, but the instinct lingers—keeping us in line, for better or worse. The trick is knowing when to lean into it and when to rewrite the script. After all, the genes that kept us alive also gave us the rebels who changed everything.

The Cost of Following the Crowd

Take a look around. How many people do you know who are stuck in jobs they hate but stay because it's "secure"? How many never pursue their dreams because they're afraid of what others might think?

They follow the crowd into:

- **Debt:** Because society normalizes spending money they don't have.
- **Unfulfilling careers:** Because they were told to "play it safe."
- **Mediocrity:** Because they never question if there's something more.

The sad truth? Most people never break free. They settle, not because they have to, but because they never dared to step outside the herd.

Real-World Examples of Thinking Differently

Success belongs to those who refuse to conform—those who think differently, challenge norms, and take bold risks.

Melanie Perkins – Building Canva Despite Industry Doubt

Melanie Perkins was just 19 years old when she saw a gap in the market—graphic design software was too complicated for the average person. While Adobe was dominating the industry, she had a bold vision: a simple, user-friendly design tool for everyone.

Experts laughed at her idea. They said graphic design couldn't be simplified. Investors turned her down over 100 times. They told her that competing with tech giants like Adobe was impossible.

But Perkins refused to listen. She and her co-founder built Canva from scratch, proving that people wanted an easier way to design. Today, Canva is valued at over $40 billion, and Perkins is one of the youngest female billionaires in the world—all because she refused to conform to industry expectations.

Steve Jobs – Rejecting the Status Quo

Steve Jobs built Apple because he refused to conform to boring, outdated technology.

- In the 1980s, computers were clunky, technical, and designed for engineers.
- Jobs ignored industry norms and focused on making user-friendly computers.
- Experts said a computer company couldn't compete by focusing on design—Jobs proved them wrong.

His refusal to conform led to the Mac, the iPod, the iPhone, and an entirely new way people interact with technology. Apple became one of the most successful companies in history—all because Jobs refused to do what everyone else was doing.

The Rise of Independent Careers

Look at the workforce today. More people than ever are leaving traditional jobs to build their own businesses, work remotely, or create digital income streams.

- Entrepreneurs, freelancers, and content creators are making millions doing what they love.
- Social media influencers, course creators, and e-commerce brands are outpacing traditional industries.
- Technology has made it possible to skip the middleman and create your own opportunities.

But most people still don't believe it's possible—because they're stuck in the old way of thinking. They don't see the new opportunities because they are too busy following outdated rules.

How to Break Free from Conformity

You cannot think like everyone else and expect to be successful. **If you want to** change your results, you must change your mindset. Here's how:

1. Question Everything

Most people never question the path they're on—they just assume it's the only way. They go to school, get a job, work for decades, and retire—because that's what they were told to do. But have you ever stopped and asked, *Is this the best path for me?*

Successful people challenge assumptions. They don't just accept the way things are—they ask:

- *Why do I believe this?*
- *Is this the best way, or just the most common way?*
- *Who benefits from me following this path?*

Example: Look at the traditional 9-to-5 job model. Millions of people believe it's the safest way to earn a living. But today, more millionaires are being created from entrepreneurship, investing, and digital businesses than ever before. The old way may be common, but is it truly the best way?

2. Stop Seeking Approval

One of the biggest reasons people conform? Fear of judgment.

- They stay in jobs they hate because they're afraid of what their family will say if they quit.
- They don't start a business because they fear criticism or failure.
- They stick to the safe, expected choices because they don't want to be seen as "different."

But here's the truth: **No one who changed the world did it by seeking approval.**

- **Steven Spielberg** was rejected by the University of Southern California's School of Cinematic Arts—twice.
- **Walt Disney** was fired for lacking imagination.
- **J.K. Rowling** was rejected 12 times before *Harry Potter* got published.

Had they listened to critics, doubters, or played it safe, they never would have achieved success. Neither will you—if you let fear of judgment control your decisions.

Action Step: Start doing **one thing every week** that pushes you outside your comfort zone, regardless of what people think. **Post a bold opinion. Apply for that**

dream job. **Start the business idea.** Stop waiting for approval.

3. Change Your Circle

You become like the people you surround yourself with. If everyone around you thinks small, plays it safe, and avoids risk, you will, too. If they complain about life but never change, you'll pick up the same habits.

But when you surround yourself with ambitious, forward-thinking people, something happens:

- You start thinking bigger.
- You begin to see new opportunities.
- You get inspired to take action.

Example: Look at the PayPal Mafia—Elon Musk, Peter Thiel, Reid Hoffman, and others. They built PayPal, then individually or through their network influenced or founded companies like Tesla, SpaceX, LinkedIn, YouTube, Yelp, and more. Why? Because they pushed each other to think beyond what was considered possible.

Action Step: Find a **new circle** of people who challenge and inspire you. **Join mastermind groups, attend networking events, and follow people online**

who are doing what you want to do. Your environment will shape your success.

4. Expose Yourself to New Ideas

If you only consume the same ideas, from the same sources, you'll never think differently. You'll keep making the same choices as everyone else.

Break out by expanding your knowledge and exposure to different ways of thinking:

- Read books on success, psychology, and finance.
- Listen to people who challenge your thinking—not just those who agree with you.
- Travel, meet new people, and step outside your routine.

Example: Warren Buffett, one of the richest men in history, spends 80% of his time reading and learning. He doesn't follow the herd—he studies, analyzes, and makes decisions based on knowledge, not emotions.

Action Step: Read **one book a month** outside your comfort zone. Expose yourself to **new industries, new ideas, and new people.** It will completely change how you see the world.

5. Take One Bold Action—Now

All the questioning, learning, and mindset shifts in the world mean nothing if you don't take action. The most powerful way to break free from conformity? Do something most people won't do.

- Work on the business idea you've been delaying.
- Invest in yourself—courses, training, coaching.
- Launch the project, take the risk, make the leap.

Most people wait for the perfect moment—but that moment never comes. Success doesn't come from waiting. It comes from action.

Action Step: Choose one major move toward your goal this week—and execute. Don't overthink it. Just do it.

Key Thought to Remember

If you want the life the majority will never have, you must do what the majority will never do.

- Don't settle for the expected path.
- Don't live by someone else's script.
- Think for yourself.

Every successful person made one key decision—to stop following and start leading. The only question is, will you?

Action Steps – Break Free from the Herd

1. **Identify areas where you conform without questioning.**
2. **Challenge one conventional belief this week.**
3. **Spend one hour a day learning something outside mainstream knowledge.**
4. **Take one action that goes against the crowd— whether it's starting a business, investing differently, or pursuing a passion others doubt.**

Final Word

If you want the life the majority will never have, you must do what the majority will never do.

- Don't settle for the expected path.
- Don't live by someone else's script.
- Think for yourself.

Every successful person made one key decision—to stop following and start leading. The only question is, will you?

CHAPTER 3:

THE POWER OF GOALS

Core Principle: *A person who has a clear goal is already on the path to success.*

Success doesn't happen by accident. It's not luck, and it's not reserved for the fortunate few. It's a byproduct of clarity, direction, and unshakable commitment to a specific target. Earl Nightingale taught that a person with a goal is like a ship with a captain—with a course charted and a destination set, success is inevitable. Without a goal, life is like a ship without a rudder—drifting, directionless, at the mercy of external forces.

The Fundamental Truth About Goal-Setting

Every major achievement in history began as a clear, specific goal—an idea transformed into a mission. The Wright brothers set out to fly before a single human had done so. Edison's goal was to create an affordable, practical lightbulb, despite thousands of failures. Every great leader, innovator, and builder was first a visionary with a defined purpose.

So why do most people wander through life without a clear direction? Because they haven't been taught the power of defining what they truly want. They let circumstances dictate their outcomes instead of setting their own course. If you don't define your goals, life will define them for you—and the results won't be in your favor.

A goal gives you a reason to wake up with purpose, to push forward when obstacles appear, and to persist when others quit. Without it, you're simply reacting to life instead of creating it.

Clarity is Power

A vague wish like *"I want to be successful"* is meaningless. Success must be defined, measured, and broken down into achievable steps. A goal like *"I will earn $100,000 in my business by December 31"* gives your mind a clear target to focus on. It triggers action. It forces you to think differently, to prioritize, to remove distractions.

Specificity is key. The more defined your goal, the more powerfully your mind works to achieve it. Napoleon Hill, in *Think and Grow Rich*, wrote: *"Definiteness of purpose is the starting point of all achievement."* Without a definite goal, your potential is wasted.

The SMART Goal Framework

To make goals **practical and achievable**, they must be:

- **Specific** – Define exactly what you want. (Not "I want to be rich," but "I will earn $500,000 through my investments.")
- **Measurable** – If you can't measure it, you can't track progress.
- **Achievable** – Be honest with yourself about how much you're willing to commit.
- **Relevant** – It must align with your long-term vision.
- **Time-bound** – Goals need deadlines to create urgency.

A well-structured goal might be: *"I will increase my business revenue by 50% within 12 months by launching a new marketing strategy and acquiring five new clients per month."* This isn't just a wish—it's a **structured plan for success.**

Real-World Examples of Goals in Action

1. **SpaceX – A Bold, Clear Mission**
   Elon Musk didn't just wish for interplanetary travel. He set a specific goal—to make humanity a multi-planetary species. Every decision at SpaceX aligns with that vision. Because of that unwavering clarity, SpaceX achieved what was once thought impossible—privately developed reusable rockets.

2. **Uber – A Precise, Disruptive Goal**
   The founders of Uber didn't vaguely hope to "improve transportation." Their goal was to make on-demand rides available in every major city worldwide. That clear mission drove their strategy, innovation, and expansion—and they disrupted an entire industry.

3. **Arnold Schwarzenegger – Visualizing and Achieving**
   Before he became an actor or governor, Schwarzenegger set a specific goal to win Mr. Olympia. He visualized it daily, trained relentlessly, and won the title seven times. When he turned to acting, he didn't just hope to get movie roles—his goal was to become the highest-paid action star in Hollywood. Each

step of his life was driven by a clear, defined goal.

The Science of Writing Down Goals – The John Goddard Story

In 1940, **John Goddard** was just 15 years old when he overheard an adult say, "If only I had done this when I was younger." That single comment shook him. He decided he would never live a life of regret, so he sat down and wrote out 127 life goals—things he wanted to accomplish, places he wanted to see, skills he wanted to master.

That list included climbing Mount Kilimanjaro, exploring the Amazon River, flying a jet, running a mile in five minutes, and reading the complete works of Shakespeare, Plato, and Aristotle. It was ambitious, specific, and personal. By the time he died in 2013, he had completed 109 of those goals — including his number one goal — becoming the first person ever to go down the 4,300 miles of the Nile River (he did it in a 15 foot kayak). Goddard lived a life few could even dream of.

What made Goddard different? He wrote his goals down. Not vague wishes, not passing dreams—clear, defined objectives. He turned thoughts into commitments, and that made all the difference.

Dr. Gail Matthews' Research – The Power of Writing Goals

Dr. Gail Matthews, a psychology professor at Dominican University of California, conducted one of the most comprehensive studies on goal-setting. She found that people who write down their goals and consistently track their progress are 42% more likely to achieve them than those who merely think about them.

Why? Because writing creates clarity and accountability. A goal in your mind is fluid, easy to forget, easy to rationalize away. A goal written on paper becomes real, structured, and measurable. It serves as a daily reminder of what you set out to do.

The Bucket List Effect

Matthews' research also highlighted something interesting—writing down life goals, like a bucket list, dramatically increases the likelihood of accomplishing them. Those who take the time to write out their long-term dreams—whether it's traveling, learning an instrument, or starting a business—are significantly more likely to make them happen.

Most people drift through life with vague ambitions—one day, they'd like to travel, write a book, or run a marathon. But without clarity, those dreams fade into the background. The ones who put them on paper and commit are the ones who turn their dreams into reality.

Success Leaves Clues

The most successful people don't leave their future to chance. They define their goals, write them down, and break them into achievable action steps. This isn't just for dreamers like John Goddard—it applies to business, health, finance, and personal fulfillment.

If you want to transform an idea into something real, write it down, review it often, and track your progress. Whether it's launching a business, improving your health, or seeing the world—what gets written, gets done.

The Think on Paper Method

1. **Write down your primary goal.** The clearer, the better.

2. **Break it into monthly milestones.** What must be done each month to stay on track?
3. **Break it into weekly steps.** What actions will move you forward each week?
4. **Daily Action.** Each morning, ask: *What's the most important thing I can do today to bring me closer to my goal?*

Overcoming Obstacles – The Reality of Goal-Setting

Every big goal faces resistance. Challenges will arise. People will doubt you. You will doubt yourself. This is where most people quit—not because their goal was impossible, but because they lacked persistence.

Consider this example:

In 1975, **Sylvester Stallone** was a struggling actor— nearly broke, living in a rough apartment, and desperate for a breakthrough. He wrote the script for *Rocky* in just three days after watching Muhammad Ali fight Chuck Wepner, inspired by the grit of an underdog. The studios loved the script—but they didn't love Stallone for the lead.

United Artists, MGM, and other studios saw potential in the film but wanted a bankable star—

actors like Robert Redford, Ryan O'Neal, or Burt Reynolds. Stallone, however, was unwavering in his vision: *Rocky Balboa had to be played by me.* He turned down a $350,000 payday—a massive sum at the time—because it meant giving up his starring role.

Producers Irwin Winkler and Robert Chartoff saw Stallone's passion and fought for him. They convinced United Artists to take a chance, but there was a condition: the budget had to be slashed from several million to just $1 million. Stallone bet on himself by accepting a small upfront salary in exchange for backend profits.

The gamble paid off. *Rocky* went on to gross $225 million worldwide, win Best Picture in 1976, and launch Stallone into stardom. His story isn't about rejection—it's about holding firm to a goal, refusing to compromise, and proving his worth when the world had doubts.

The difference between success and failure isn't talent—it's the ability to keep going when most people stop.

Action Steps – Setting and Achieving Your Goal

1. Write down one specific goal for the next 12 months.
2. Break it down into monthly, weekly, and daily action steps.
3. Review your progress every Sunday. Adjust as needed.
4. Visualize your goal as already achieved—daily.
5. Commit to unwavering persistence—no matter what obstacles arise.

The Final Word

A person with a goal is **unstoppable**. They wake up each day **with purpose, direction, and drive**. Without a goal, life is aimless—reacting instead of creating. Set your goal. Commit to it. Take action daily.

This is the power of goal-setting. It will determine the future you create.

CHAPTER 4:

SUCCESS AS THE PROGRESSIVE REALIZATION OF A WORTHY IDEAL

Core Principle: *Success isn't a destination—it's the ongoing pursuit of a meaningful goal.*

Most people misunderstand success. They see it as a finish line, a point in the future where they will finally "have it all." They believe that once they accumulate enough money, the right job, or the perfect lifestyle, they will have "made it." But that's not how success works.

Earl Nightingale gave us the simplest, yet most profound definition of success:

> "Success is the progressive realization of a worthy ideal."

Let that sink in—progressive realization. Success is not a final achievement. It is an ongoing pursuit of a goal that is both meaningful and worthy to the individual. If you are working toward something that excites you, challenges you, and makes you better, you are already successful.

The problem? Most people never define their own worthy ideal. They chase someone else's version of success. They follow the expectations of society, family, and peer pressure without asking, *Is this what I really want?* That's why so many people feel unfulfilled, even after achieving what they thought they wanted.

The Importance of Defining Success for Yourself

You can spend your life chasing things that don't fulfill you simply because you never stopped to think about what success really means to you.

Society teaches people that success looks like:

- A high-paying corporate job
- A big house in the right neighborhood
- A luxury car and designer clothes
- A long list of accomplishments that impress others

But ask yourself: *Do these things actually align with my values?*

Success isn't one-size-fits-all. It is deeply personal. A high-powered lawyer earning millions may be miserable, while a teacher earning a modest salary feels completely fulfilled. The difference? The teacher is living in alignment with their purpose.

Here's the truth: If you don't define success for yourself, the world will define it for you. And more often than not, you'll spend your life chasing a version of success that leaves you empty and exhausted.

Success is a Journey, Not a Destination

The biggest mistake people make is believing they will be happy when they "arrive."

- *"I'll be successful when I make six figures."*
- *"I'll be happy when I buy my dream house."*
- *"I'll feel fulfilled when I finally retire."*

But the finish line never arrives. The moment you achieve one goal, another appears. People who define success as a static endpoint end up disillusioned. They reach their goal, but instead of feeling satisfied, they feel lost.

Success isn't about reaching a final point—it's about constant growth and movement toward something meaningful.

Think about the greatest achievers in history. Did they stop once they reached a certain milestone? No. They kept pushing, innovating, and expanding their vision. They understood that the pursuit itself was the success.

Real-World Examples of Success as a Journey

1. Richard Branson – Building for the Challenge, Not Just the Money

Richard Branson didn't set out to build a billion-dollar empire—he set out to pursue exciting, meaningful challenges.

- He started Virgin Records at 20 years old because he loved music.
- He launched Virgin Atlantic because he wanted to improve air travel.
- He created Virgin Galactic because space exploration excited him.

Every venture was a new journey, not an endpoint. Branson's success is measured not by his net worth, but by his constant pursuit of new frontiers.

2. Maya Angelou – A Lifetime of Impact Through Words

Maya Angelou's success wasn't about fame or fortune—it was about expressing truth through storytelling.

- She was a poet, civil rights activist, author, and speaker—and never stopped creating.
- She wrote over 30 books, each one a step in her lifelong journey of impacting others.
- Even after global recognition, she continued to mentor, teach, and inspire.

Her success was not in one book, one speech, or one award—it was the constant pursuit of her mission to give voice to the unheard.

3. Jeff Bezos – The Amazon Journey

Jeff Bezos didn't start Amazon to become the richest man in the world—he started it because he saw a huge opportunity for innovation.

- He started by selling books online from his garage.
- He expanded Amazon into a global e-commerce powerhouse.
- He moved into cloud computing, AI, and space exploration with Blue Origin.

Bezos didn't stop at one success—he continuously evolved and expanded his vision. That's what made him successful—not just the money, but the relentless pursuit of new frontiers.

The Role of Failure in Success

If success is progress toward a worthy ideal, then failure is simply proof that you are in motion. Every great achievement in history is built on a foundation of setbacks, rejections, and missteps. The difference between those who succeed and those who don't is simple: successful people do not see failure as the end—they see it as feedback.

Too many people let temporary failure turn into permanent defeat. They hit a wall, experience rejection, or face setbacks, and they quit. But the truth is, failure is not the opposite of success—it is part of it. Every failure is a lesson. Every setback is an opportunity to refine, adjust, and keep moving forward.

Let's look at some of the greatest examples of failure turned into success.

Howard Schultz – Rejected 242 Times Before Starbucks Took Off

Howard Schultz didn't come from wealth. He grew up in a working-class neighborhood in Brooklyn, where his father struggled to make ends meet. When Schultz discovered a small coffee shop in Seattle called Starbucks, he saw an opportunity—to bring Italian-style coffee culture to America.

But there was one problem: investors didn't believe in his vision.

Schultz was turned down 242 times while trying to raise money to expand Starbucks. Again and again, he was told:

- *"Americans will never pay $4 for a cup of coffee."*
- *"Coffee shops aren't a viable business model."*
- *"It's a niche idea—it won't work on a large scale."*

He could have quit. He could have accepted their version of reality. But he didn't. He kept pitching, kept refining his message, and kept believing. Finally, he secured the funding he needed—and Starbucks grew from a single store into a global empire with over 35,000 locations.

Lesson: If Schultz had quit after his first 10, 50, or even 200 rejections, Starbucks would not exist today. Success requires persistence in the face of doubt.

Vera Wang – From Olympic Dreams to Fashion Icon

Vera Wang had one dream growing up: to be an Olympic figure skater. She trained for years, sacrificing time, energy, and effort, all for one goal—competing at the highest level. But despite her dedication, she failed to make the U.S. Olympic team.

At 19, her dream was over. She had spent her entire childhood working toward something that would never happen.

Many people would have stopped there, defeated. But Wang didn't dwell on what was lost—she focused on what was next. She pivoted to journalism, then fashion, and eventually became an editor at *Vogue*.

At age 40—when most designers were already established—she launched her own fashion line. Today, she is one of the most successful and respected designers in the world, known for revolutionizing bridal fashion.

Lesson: Failure is not an endpoint—it's a redirection. Wang's Olympic dream didn't materialize, but that didn't mean she wasn't meant for greatness. Your failures often point you toward your true calling.

Travis Kalanick – From Scandal to Redemption

Travis Kalanick was one of the most aggressive and ambitious entrepreneurs in Silicon Valley. As the co-founder of Uber, he disrupted the entire transportation industry, growing the company into a global powerhouse.

But success wasn't smooth.

By 2017, Uber was plagued by scandals—accusations of toxic workplace culture, regulatory battles, driver disputes, and sexual harassment claims. Kalanick was forced to resign as CEO of the company he built. His name was tarnished, and many believed his career was over.

But like all great entrepreneurs, he didn't let failure define him.

Instead of disappearing, Kalanick quietly started over. He launched CloudKitchens, a company that builds kitchen spaces for delivery-only restaurants. Many laughed at the idea—but within a few years, it was valued at over $15 billion.

He didn't let one setback destroy his drive, ambition, or vision. He learned, adapted, and built again.

Lesson: Even the most successful people experience failure, criticism, and rejection. What matters is how you respond. Do you let failure define you? Or do you use it as fuel to create something even greater?

What These Stories Teach Us

1. **Failure is not final.** It's just part of the process.
2. **Rejection doesn't mean you're wrong—it means you need to persist.**
3. **Setbacks often point you toward a bigger, better path.**
4. **Success isn't about avoiding failure—it's about how you handle it.**

Think about your own life. Have you let a failure stop you? Have you quit on something because of rejection or setbacks? If so, now is the time to change your perspective.

Action Steps: Turning Failure into Fuel for Success

1. **Reframe failure as feedback.** What did this setback teach you?

2. **Look for the opportunity within the obstacle.** What's the next step?
3. **Commit to persistence.** If something is truly important to you, keep going.
4. **Surround yourself with examples of resilience.** Study people who overcame failure and came out stronger.

Failure is not the opposite of success. It is the road to success. The only way you lose is if you stop walking the path.

How to Define and Pursue Your Worthy Ideal

Success isn't accidental—it is built with deliberate clarity and daily action.

1. Define Your Worthy Ideal

- Ask yourself, *What excites me?*
- *What kind of work would I do for free?*
- *If money wasn't an issue, how would I spend my time?*

Your ideal must be deeply personal. Not what your parents want, not what society expects—what truly fuels you.

2. Take Consistent Action

A dream without action is just a wish. To make progress:

- Set specific, measurable goals.
- Break them into daily steps.
- Develop habits that align with success.

A writer writes every day.
An athlete trains every day.
An entrepreneur builds every day.

Progress, not perfection, is the key.

3. Track Your Progress and Adjust

If success is a journey, not a destination, then you must adjust your course as you go.

- Track small wins.
- Evaluate your direction every 90 days.
- Celebrate progress, not just outcomes.

Success is not about hitting one big goal—it's about staying in motion, refining, and growing over time.

Action Steps – Living a Successful Life

1. **Write down your personal definition of success.**

2. Identify one major goal that aligns with your worthy ideal.
3. Break that goal into daily and weekly action steps.
4. Take one meaningful action today.
5. Celebrate progress, no matter how small.

Final Thought

Success isn't a number, a title, or an endpoint—it's the daily pursuit of a life that excites and fulfills you.

- A scientist in the lab, solving problems, is successful.
- A musician, creating music that moves people, is successful.
- A business owner, building something bigger than themselves, is successful.

As long as you are progressing toward your worthy ideal, you are already successful.

Now, the only question is: What's your worthy ideal? And are you moving toward it today?

CHAPTER 5:
THE SCIENCE OF HABITS

Core Principle: Our habits determine our future.

Take a look at your daily routine. The small, repeated actions you take—what you eat, how you spend your time, the thoughts you entertain, the work you do—are shaping your future. Whether you succeed or fail, grow or stagnate, thrive or struggle depends not on big, dramatic moments, but on the tiny choices you make every day.

Earl Nightingale understood this truth: "You will become what you think about most of the time." But here's an extension of that truth—what you repeatedly do becomes who you are.

Most people don't control their habits. They wake up, grab their phone, check the news, scroll through social media, rush through their morning, and spend their days reacting to life instead of building it deliberately. Then they wonder why they feel stuck.

Success is never an accident. It is built on the back of disciplined, productive habits. The most successful people in the world are not necessarily smarter or more talented—they have simply mastered their daily routines.

If you control your habits, you control your destiny.

Why Habits Matter More Than Motivation

Most people believe they need more motivation to succeed. They wait for inspiration to strike. They think successful people wake up every day feeling driven, energized, and ready to go. But that's not the truth.

The most successful people in the world don't rely on motivation—they rely on habits.

Motivation is temporary. It's a feeling, and like all feelings, it comes and goes. One day, you wake up excited to work out, eat healthy, or build your business. The next day, you're tired, unmotivated, and tempted to skip it. If motivation is all you have, you'll fail—because you can't control your emotions.

Habits, on the other hand, are automatic. They don't require motivation. Once a habit is locked in, it runs on autopilot. You don't think about brushing your teeth, tying your shoes, or driving to work—you just do it. Imagine if your success habits were that automatic.

A motivated person might go to the gym when they feel like it. A person with the habit of training shows up every day, no matter what.

A motivated writer waits for inspiration. A writer with a habit sits down and writes, even when it's hard.

A motivated entrepreneur works when excited. A successful entrepreneur builds daily, even through setbacks.

That's the secret. Motivation fades. Habits stay. If you master your habits, success becomes inevitable.

How Habits Are Formed: The Habit Loop

Every habit—good or bad—follows the same pattern. It's not random. It's a loop, running on autopilot in your brain. Once you understand this, you can take control of your habits instead of being controlled by them.

The **Habit Loop** consists of three steps:

1. **Cue (Trigger):** The event that starts the habit.
2. **Routine (Action):** The behavior you perform.
3. **Reward (Outcome):** The benefit your brain receives, reinforcing the habit.

Example: The Coffee Habit

- **Cue:** You wake up and feel tired.
- **Routine:** You make a cup of coffee.
- **Reward:** You feel more awake.

Your brain learns: *When I feel tired (cue), I drink coffee (routine), and I feel better (reward).* Do it enough times, and it becomes **automatic**—no thinking required.

This is how bad habits form. You feel stressed (cue), eat junk food (routine), feel momentary relief (reward)—and the loop repeats. The good news? You can reprogram any habit.

Want to build a new habit?

- **Attach it to an existing cue.** (Example: After brushing your teeth, do 10 push-ups.)
- **Make the reward clear.** (Example: Track your progress—success itself is motivating.)
- **Repeat daily until it's automatic.**

Once a habit is wired in, motivation isn't needed. Your brain runs the loop without effort. Master the loop, and you master your future.

Real-World Examples of Habits Shaping Success

Success isn't about luck, talent, or intelligence. It's about habits. The people who achieve extraordinary things don't wait for motivation or inspiration—they build routines that guarantee success. Day after day, they follow the same disciplined habits, and over time, those habits create unstoppable momentum.

Let's look at three individuals who used the power of habit to rise to the top.

1. James Clear – The Power of Small Daily Habits

James Clear didn't start as an expert on habit formation. He was a college baseball player who suffered a traumatic brain injury after being hit in the face with a bat. His recovery was slow and grueling, but it taught him one critical lesson: the power of small, consistent improvements.

Instead of chasing big, dramatic changes, Clear focused on tiny habits—just 1% better every day. He rebuilt his life using:

- Daily writing habits that eventually led to his best-selling book, *Atomic Habits*.
- Consistent fitness habits that transformed his body and mindset.
- Simple routines that compounded into massive success.

Today, his work has helped millions of people break bad habits, build productive ones, and rewire their lives for success. His core principle? You don't need massive willpower—you just need better systems.

Success isn't about motivation. It's about setting up habits that make success inevitable.

2. Kobe Bryant – The Relentless Pursuit of Excellence

Kobe Bryant wasn't just one of the greatest basketball players of all time—he was one of the most disciplined individuals to ever play the game. His success wasn't an accident. It was built on ruthless, consistent habits.

Bryant's work ethic was legendary. While other players showed up for practice, he was already on the court at 4:00 AM, shooting hundreds of jumpers before his teammates even arrived. His philosophy? Outwork everyone—every day.

Here's how Bryant's habits shaped his success:

- Extreme early morning training: He often started before sunrise, putting in extra hours before regular team practices even began.
- Brutal practice discipline: He would perform the same move thousands of times, ensuring perfection.
- Film study obsession: He spent hours reviewing game footage, studying opponents' weaknesses and refining his skills.
- Unshakable commitment to improvement: Even after winning five NBA championships, he still trained like a rookie trying to prove himself.

Bryant didn't just rely on talent. He made winning a habit. His daily routines ensured his dominance, and his legacy as one of the greatest basketball players in history was built one disciplined day at a time.

The lesson? Success doesn't come from occasional bursts of effort—it comes from the daily grind of disciplined habits.

3. Warren Buffett – The Habit of Lifelong Learning

Warren Buffett isn't the richest man in the world because of luck. His success comes from one fundamental habit—learning.

Buffett spends 80% of his day reading and thinking. While most people chase short-term gains, he plays the long game, focusing on continuous improvement and deep knowledge.

His habits include:

- Reading 500 pages a day. He believes knowledge compounds just like money—the more you learn, the more you earn.
- Avoiding emotional decision-making. He doesn't react impulsively—he makes calculated, informed choices.
- Following a strict investing discipline. He doesn't chase trends—he sticks to what works.

Buffett's wealth isn't the result of one lucky investment—it's the product of decades of learning, thinking, and applying knowledge.

The Common Theme: Habits Build Success

These three individuals—James Clear, Kobe Bryant, and Warren Buffett—achieved success in different fields, but they all followed the same formula:

1. They designed their days for success.
2. They followed disciplined routines, no matter what.

3. They focused on small, daily improvements.

You don't need more motivation—you need better habits. Build the right routines, and success will take care of itself.

How to Build Life-Changing Habits

Want to transform your life? Don't rely on motivation. **Instead,** install habits that make success inevitable.

Here's how:

1. Start Small – The 2-Minute Rule

Most people fail at new habits because they try to do too much too fast. Instead, shrink your habit to two minutes or less so it's easy to do.

- Want to read more? Read one page per day.
- Want to exercise? Do one push-up.
- Want to write a book? Write one sentence.

These small actions eliminate resistance and build momentum.

2. Stack Habits – Attach a New Habit to an Old One

You already have habits. Use them to create new ones.

- After I brush my teeth, I will read one page of a book.
- After I pour my morning coffee, I will write down three goals.
- After I finish lunch, I will take a five-minute walk.

This method makes new habits automatic—because they piggyback off old ones.

3. Design Your Environment for Success

You don't need more willpower—you need **a** better setup.

- Want to eat healthy? Keep junk food out of your house.
- Want to work out? Lay out your gym clothes the night before.
- Want to focus? Turn off notifications and remove distractions.

Your environment should make good habits easy and bad habits hard.

4. Track Progress – The Power of Streaks

Progress fuels motivation. Track your habits so you don't break the chain.

- Use a habit tracker or a simple notebook.

- Mark an "X" for every day you complete your habit.
- Watch the streak grow—and don't break it.

Even small wins create momentum that keeps you going.

The Habit Formula for Success

Want to install a new habit? Follow this simple formula:

1. **Make it obvious.** (Set up cues and reminders.)
2. **Make it easy.** (Start small—2 minutes or less.)
3. **Make it rewarding.** (Track progress and celebrate wins.)
4. **Make it consistent.** (Never miss two days in a row.)

If you do this, success will become automatic.

Missed a Day? FIDO - Forget It, Drive On

You will fail. Let's get that out of the way. You will miss a day. You will fall off track. You will slip back into old habits. That's not the problem. The problem is what you do next.

Most people make failure bigger than it is. They miss a workout and think, *Well, I blew it. Might as well quit.*

They skip a writing session and say, *Guess I'm not a writer after all.* They eat one bad meal and decide, *I'll start again next month.*

That's the trap. Failure is never final—unless you let it be.

Clebe McClary, a former Marine who survived devastating battlefield injuries, had a saying: FIDO—Forget It, Drive On. In war, hesitation means death. If you make a mistake, you don't sit there and dwell on it—you correct course and move forward.

The same applies to your habits. Missed a day? Forget it, drive on.

- Skipped a workout? Get back to it tomorrow.
- Fell off your diet? Your next meal is a new start.
- Missed a work session? Pick up right where you left off.

One misstep doesn't erase all your progress. What ruins people isn't failure—it's letting failure become their excuse to quit.

Success isn't about perfection. It's about consistency. If you fall, get up. If you miss, reset. Forget it. Drive on. That's how you win.

Action Steps: Take Control of Your Habits Today

1. **Identify one bad habit** holding you back.
2. **Decide on one new habit** that moves you toward your goals.
3. Start small—shrink it to 2 minutes.
4. Stack it onto an existing habit.
5. Track your progress daily.

Final Thought

Your habits are either **building your future or destroying it.**

- Every meal is a vote for your health or against it.
- Every dollar spent is a step toward wealth or debt.
- Every choice moves you closer to success or further from it.

Your future is hidden in your daily routine. Control your habits, and you control your destiny.

CHAPTER 6:

THE ROLE OF SERVICE

Core Principle: The key to prosperity is service.

Look around at the most successful people, the greatest businesses, and the wealthiest entrepreneurs. What do they have in common? They serve others. They provide value. They solve problems.

Earl Nightingale made it clear:

> **"Our rewards in life will always be in exact proportion to our service."**

Most people get this backward. They chase money without offering anything of real value. They expect success without providing something useful to others. But wealth, fulfillment, and lasting achievement are always the result of service.

If you want more success, stop focusing on what you can get and start focusing on what you can give.

Why Service Determines Success

Success is not about what you can get—it's about what you can give. The more you serve, the more valuable you become. The more valuable you become, the greater your rewards. It's a simple formula, yet most people miss it.

Think about the most successful businesses in the world. Amazon dominates because it makes life easier for customers. Apple thrives because it creates products that people love. The best restaurants, the best professionals, the best leaders—they all succeed by serving others exceptionally well.

Now, look at those who struggle. They are often focused on themselves—what they can take, what they can gain, what they are owed. But success doesn't work that way. Money follows value. Opportunity follows service.

If you want to earn more, serve more. If you want to advance in your career, make yourself indispensable. If you want a thriving business, solve a real problem for people. Success is the result of service.

Ask yourself: How can I bring more value today? That question alone will change your life. The moment you stop chasing success and start focusing on helping others succeed, success will start chasing you. That's the law. That's the key. Give more, serve better, and watch your life transform.

The Mindset of Service vs. Selfishness

There are two types of people in this world: those who serve and those who take.

The people who struggle—who feel stuck, frustrated, and unfulfilled—operate with a mindset of taking. They focus on what they can get, what they deserve, and what others should do for them. They ask questions like:

- *Why am I not getting paid more?*
- *Why aren't people recognizing my efforts?*
- *Why isn't life giving me what I want?*

This mindset leads to resentment, stagnation, and disappointment. Why? Because success doesn't come from demanding more—it comes from giving more.

Now, look at the people who thrive. They think differently. Instead of asking, *What can I get?*, they ask:

- How can I create more value?
- How can I help others win?

- How can I make myself indispensable?

These are the people who advance. They get promoted, build wealth, and create lasting impact. Not because they chase success, but because they serve their way to it.

The world rewards those who contribute more than they take. Every great leader, business owner, and innovator built their success by focusing on service first. The moment you shift from expecting to contributing, everything changes.

The choice is yours: Will you demand more or serve more? One leads to frustration. The other leads to success.

The world rewards those who give more than they take.

Real-World Examples of Service Leading to Success

1. Bass Pro Shops – Serving Customers, Not Just Selling Products

Johnny Morris, the founder of Bass Pro Shops, didn't start by trying to build a billion-dollar company. He started by serving a need.

- As an avid fisherman, he realized that quality fishing gear was hard to find.
- Instead of complaining, he took action—selling the best fishing tackle out of his father's liquor store.
- His focus wasn't just on making money—it was on providing the best products and experience for fellow fishermen.

Because of this, Bass Pro Shops grew into a massive outdoor retailer, generating billions in revenue. Why? Because it put service first.

Lesson: Focus on serving a need, not just making money. The money follows the service.

2. TOMS Shoes – The One-for-One Model of Giving

Blake Mycoskie didn't start TOMS Shoes just to sell footwear. He built it with a mission to serve.

- He saw that millions of children around the world lacked proper shoes.
- Instead of just creating another shoe brand, he launched the One-for-One model—for every pair sold, TOMS donated a pair to a child in need.
- His company didn't just make money—it made an impact.

The result? A wildly successful global brand that proved business could be about service first, profit second.

Lesson: The best businesses don't just sell—they serve.

3. Sam Walton – Obsessed with Customer Service

Sam Walton, the founder of Walmart, became one of the wealthiest men in history. But his success didn't come from trying to get rich—it came from an obsession with serving customers.

- He personally walked the aisles of his stores, talking to customers, asking how he could improve.
- He built Walmart around low prices and convenience, focusing on how he could provide more value.
- He believed in putting customers first—always.

Because of his relentless focus on service, Walmart became the largest retailer in the world.

Lesson: The best way to win in business? Serve your customers better than anyone else.

The Service Formula for Success

Success is not complicated. It follows a simple formula:

1. **Find a problem people have.**
2. **Solve it better than anyone else.**
3. **Do it consistently with excellence.**

That's it. That's the key to success in business, careers, and life.

Look at the most successful businesses. They solve problems.

- Amazon makes shopping easier.
- Apple makes technology simple and elegant.
- FedEx makes shipping fast and reliable.

Look at the most successful people. They bring value.

- A top employee makes their boss's job easier.
- A great leader serves their team, not just themselves.
- The best entrepreneurs obsess over their customers.

And look at those who struggle. They focus on what they can get, not what they can give. They demand more without offering more. They miss the formula.

Want to get ahead? Stop chasing money. Stop asking what the world owes you. Instead, ask: How can I serve more? How can I provide more value?

The moment you shift your focus from taking to giving, everything changes. The better you serve, the greater your rewards. That's the law. That's the formula. Master it, and success is inevitable.

How to Make Service a Habit

Success doesn't come from one-time acts of service—it comes from making service a way of life. The people who win in business, careers, and relationships don't serve occasionally—they serve daily.

But here's the problem: Most people think of service as extra effort, something to do when they "have time." They treat it as a nice idea, not a way of operating.

That's why they stay stuck.

If you want to succeed at the highest level, service must become a habit—something you do without thinking, something built into your daily actions.

Here's how you make that happen:

1. Shift Your Focus – Ask Better Questions

Your mind is always searching for answers. If you ask weak questions—*Why am I not getting ahead? Why aren't people recognizing me?*—you get weak answers.

Instead, train yourself to ask powerful questions daily:

- **How can I create more value today?**
- **Who can I help right now?**
- **How can I make life easier for someone else?**

When you start your day focused on giving instead of taking, you shift into a mindset of service. And when service becomes your focus, success follows naturally.

2. Overdeliver in Everything You Do

Average people do the minimum. Successful people do more than expected.

- Employees who go the extra mile don't have to beg for raises—they become invaluable.
- Businesses that overdeliver don't have to chase customers—people come to them.
- Leaders who serve their teams earn loyalty, not just obedience.

Train yourself to do more than what's required. If you see a problem, solve it. If you notice a need, fill it. If someone expects a little, give them a lot.

When you become the person who always overdelivers, opportunities chase you.

3. Build Service into Your Routine

If something isn't in your routine, it won't last. To make service a habit, tie it to your daily schedule.

- Start your day with a service mindset. Write down one way you can help someone today.
- At work, make service automatic. Ask, "How can I improve things here?" and act on it.
- In your relationships, give before you take. Whether in business, friendships, or marriage, make it a habit to serve first.

The more you integrate service into your day, the more natural it becomes. Soon, you won't have to think about it—it will just be who you are.

4. Serve Without Keeping Score

Most people serve with expectations. They do something nice and immediately wonder, *What's in it for me?* That's not service—that's a transaction.

True service is giving without looking for payback. Ironically, those who serve without expecting rewards are the ones who end up receiving the most.

Make it a habit to help, give, and contribute without worrying about the return. The rewards will come—but they'll come naturally, not because you demanded them.

Final Thought: Success Follows Service

Your life and business will rise to the level of your service. **Make service a habit, and success will take care of itself.** Start today. Give more. Serve better. Watch your world change.

CHAPTER 7:

GRATITUDE UNLEASHED – THE HIDDEN POWER THAT CHANGES EVERYTHING

Core Principle: *Gratitude isn't just a feeling—it's a force that transforms your mind, your actions, and your outcomes.*

Gratitude is often misunderstood. Most people think of it as something you practice when things are going well—when life is good, the bank account is full, and everything is falling into place. But true gratitude isn't just about appreciating the good times—it's about training yourself to find the good, even in the hardest moments.

Earl Nightingale understood this principle well. He said:

"We tend to live up to our expectations."

Gratitude shifts those expectations. It forces your mind to focus on what's already working, already abundant, already valuable in your life—and in doing so, it expands those things.

Think about it:

- The more you appreciate your opportunities, the more opportunities you create.
- The more you focus on what's going right, the more right things seem to happen.
- The more you recognize what you already have, the more value you get from it.

Gratitude is not passive—it is an active power that rewires your brain, changes your decisions, and opens doors you never saw before.

Why Gratitude is the Key to Unlocking a Better Life

Science now confirms what the great thinkers have always known: gratitude changes everything.

- It rewires the brain for positivity. Studies show that regularly practicing gratitude strengthens neural pathways associated with happiness and success.

- It reduces stress and anxiety. Gratitude forces the mind to focus on what's right instead of what's wrong.
- It creates resilience. When challenges arise, a grateful mind sees lessons instead of losses, opportunities instead of obstacles.
- It builds stronger relationships. People who express gratitude are more likable, trustworthy, and magnetic.

But here's the real key: **Gratitude is not just about emotion—it's about action.**

The people who lead the best lives are not just grateful in their hearts—they use gratitude to take bold action, to give more, to create more, to expand their world.

Let's look at how gratitude transforms lives, businesses, and entire industries.

Real-World Examples of Gratitude in Action

1. Sara Blakely – From Failure to Billionaire by Embracing Gratitude

Sara Blakely, the founder of Spanx, built her empire on gratitude, not bitterness.

Before Spanx, she was selling fax machines door-to-door, facing constant rejection. But instead of becoming resentful, she made gratitude her mental strategy.

- Every time a door slammed in her face, she told herself, "This is a lesson. This is preparing me for something bigger."
- When she started Spanx, she handwrote thank-you notes to every customer, investor, and supporter.
- She credits her success not to avoiding failure, but to being grateful for it—because it taught her persistence, resilience, and creativity.

Gratitude didn't just change her attitude—it changed her outcomes.

2. Kayleigh McEnany – Gratitude Amidst Challenges

Kayleigh McEnany, former White House Press Secretary and television commentator, has openly shared how gratitude and faith shaped her journey—especially during adversity.

- Before achieving success, she faced serious health challenges, including a BRCA1 gene mutation that led her to undergo a preventative double mastectomy in her 20s.

Instead of dwelling on fear, she focused on gratitude for medical advancements and the opportunity to take control of her health.
- During her time as Press Secretary, she was heavily scrutinized and faced relentless media attacks. But rather than allowing criticism to consume her, she maintained a mindset of gratitude—for her faith, her opportunities, and the chance to serve.
- She has credited her deep gratitude for God's plan in her life as the reason she remained steady under pressure and optimistic despite challenges.

Her story is a reminder that gratitude is not just for the easy moments—it's the fuel that keeps you going through the toughest battles.

3. Walt Disney – Seeing Possibility Instead of Setbacks

Walt Disney's early years were filled with failure and rejection—he was fired from a newspaper for "lacking imagination," his first company went bankrupt, and he was turned down hundreds of times trying to get funding for Disneyland.

But he remained grateful for the vision he had—and for every setback, because it pushed him forward.

- Instead of focusing on rejection, he focused on what he still had—a dream worth fighting for.
- Instead of dwelling on losses, he used them as fuel to work harder and prove people wrong.
- His gratitude for creativity, storytelling, and bringing joy to others built one of the most powerful brands in history.

Gratitude didn't just make Disney optimistic—it made him unstoppable.

By shifting from complaint to gratitude, from setbacks to lessons, from obstacles to stepping stones, these individuals turned adversity into achievement. Gratitude was their anchor—what will it be for you?

Gratitude Connects You With Your Creator

Gratitude isn't just a tool for success—it's a spiritual force that connects you with something greater than yourself. Across history, in every major faith and spiritual tradition, gratitude is seen as a direct path to wisdom, peace, and divine connection.

Why? Because gratitude shifts the heart from self-centeredness to humility, from entitlement to appreciation, from fear to trust. When you recognize that life itself is a gift, that every breath, every opportunity, every moment is something given to you—your perspective changes.

Gratitude isn't just about acknowledging the good in your life. It's about recognizing the source of that good. And every major faith teaches that gratitude is the key to a deeper relationship with the Divine.

What the World's Major Faiths Teach About Gratitude

Christianity: "Give Thanks in All Circumstances"

The Bible is filled with **commands to be grateful, not just in good times, but in all situations.**

"Give thanks in all circumstances; for this is God's will for you in Christ Jesus." – 1 Thessalonians 5:18

Gratitude in Christianity is not just a response to blessings—it is an act of faith. It acknowledges that God is always working, even in struggles. When believers express gratitude, they align themselves with God's purpose, choosing trust over worry, faith over fear.

Jesus Himself modeled gratitude—thanking God before performing miracles, before meals, before major moments. Gratitude was not just something He taught—it was something He lived.

Lesson: Gratitude strengthens faith and deepens trust in God's plan, even when life doesn't make sense.

Islam: "If You Are Grateful, I Will Increase You"

In Islam, gratitude (*shukr*) is a central theme of faith and daily life. The Quran repeatedly reminds believers that gratitude leads to abundance and blessings.

> "If you are grateful, I will surely increase you [in favor]; but if you deny, indeed, My punishment is severe." – Quran 14:7

Gratitude in Islam is not just about feeling thankful—it's about expressing that gratitude through action. Muslims are encouraged to show gratitude to God through prayer, charity, and service to others.

The Prophet Muhammad was known for his deep gratitude. Even when faced with hardship, he remained thankful, often praying through the night in gratitude to God.

Lesson: Gratitude in action leads to spiritual and material increase.

Judaism: "Gratitude is the Foundation of Worship"

The Hebrew Bible and Jewish tradition emphasize gratitude as the foundation of faith. The very first words a Jewish person says upon waking are **"Modeh Ani"—I give thanks.**

> **"Give thanks to the Lord, for He is good; His love endures forever."** – Psalm 136:1

Jewish prayers are filled with expressions of gratitude—for food, for health, for wisdom, for simply being alive. The word "Jew" itself comes from the Hebrew word Yehudah, meaning "to give thanks."

In Judaism, gratitude is a discipline, a daily practice, a way of seeing life. It is about recognizing that everything—from the smallest blessing to the greatest miracle—is a gift.

Lesson: Gratitude is the highest form of worship—it acknowledges God as the ultimate provider.

Hinduism: "Gratitude Aligns You With the Universe"

Hindu philosophy teaches that gratitude is a spiritual force that aligns you with Dharma—the universal order.

> **"A person who is grateful gains the favor of the Divine and grows in wisdom."** – Bhagavad Gita

Gratitude is deeply tied to the concept of karma—what you put into the world comes back to you. A grateful heart attracts more abundance, while ingratitude creates suffering.

Hindu practices, such as offering food to the Divine before eating and expressing thanks in daily prayers, reinforce gratitude as a way of life.

Lesson: Gratitude creates harmony with the universe and brings inner peace.

Buddhism: "Gratitude Leads to Enlightenment"

Buddhism teaches that gratitude is a path to spiritual awakening. Instead of focusing on what's lacking, gratitude turns attention to what is present, leading to contentment and wisdom.

> **"A wise person is grateful and thankful. This protects them from greed, resentment, and suffering."** – Buddha

Buddhist monks practice gratitude daily, giving thanks for even the smallest things—a meal, a kind word, a simple breath. Gratitude removes attachment and suffering, allowing inner peace to flourish.

Lesson: Gratitude leads to detachment from suffering and deeper spiritual awareness.

The Universal Power of Gratitude

Though these traditions come from different cultures, different books, and different histories, they all point to the same truth:

Gratitude is a spiritual key that unlocks peace, wisdom, and divine connection.

Regardless of your belief system, gratitude:

- **Shifts your focus from lack to abundance.**
- **Reinforces faith in something bigger than yourself.**
- **Removes fear, worry, and doubt.**

When you practice gratitude, you move from self-reliance to divine trust. You recognize that life is not just about what you create—but also about what you've been given.

And when you acknowledge the gifts in your life, you open yourself up to receive even more.

The Ultimate Power of Gratitude: A Strong Finish

Gratitude isn't just something you do once in a while—it's something you live. It's the key to a fulfilled life, a resilient mind, and a heart that's open to success.

When you practice gratitude, you don't just change your thoughts—you change your actions. You shift from complaining to creating, from worrying to trusting, from scarcity to abundance.

Gratitude isn't passive—it's the most active force you can cultivate.

- **It deepens faith.** When you start with gratitude, you acknowledge that life is not just about what you control but about something bigger than yourself.
- **It replaces fear with trust.** Instead of feeling like life is working against you, gratitude reminds you that life is always working for you.
- **It aligns you with wisdom, peace, and divine favor.** Gratitude connects you with God, the universe, or whatever higher power you believe in—because it acknowledges the **gift of existence itself.**

Regardless of where you are on your spiritual journey, one truth remains:

A grateful heart is always closer to the Divine.

The most successful, fulfilled people aren't those who have it easy. They're the ones who find something to be grateful for, even in difficulty. They don't wait for gratitude to come naturally—they train themselves to see the good, no matter what.

Make gratitude a way of life, not just an occasional thought.

How to Make Gratitude a Daily Habit

If gratitude has the power to transform lives, why do so few people practice it? Simple: They assume it should happen naturally.

It doesn't.

Gratitude is a discipline. It's a habit. It's something you train yourself to do until it becomes second nature.

Here's how to make gratitude an active force in your life:

1. Start Your Day with a Gratitude List

Every morning, **write down three things you're grateful for.** They don't have to be big—just specific.

- Not "I'm grateful for life." Instead, *"I'm grateful for the coffee I'm drinking, the warm sunlight, and the opportunity to learn today."*

- Not "I'm grateful for my job." Instead, *"I'm grateful for the one client who trusted me this week."*

Why? Because gratitude grows when you notice the small things. The more specific you are, the more powerful it becomes.

2. Reframe Every Challenge with Gratitude

The next time you face a problem, stop and ask: **What's good about this? What can I learn?**

- **Got rejected?** Be grateful—it's making you tougher.
- **Lost an opportunity?** Be grateful—it's creating space for something better.
- **Struggling in business?** Be grateful—it's forcing you to sharpen your skills.

When you reframe failure as a gift, it loses its power over you.

3. Express Gratitude to Others – Daily

Gratitude isn't just about **what you feel—it's about what you express.**

Make it a habit to:

- **Send one thank-you message every day**—to a friend, a mentor, an employee.

- Tell people exactly what you appreciate about them.
- Acknowledge effort, not just results.

People remember who appreciates them. The more gratitude you express, the more your relationships—and opportunities—expand.

4. Use Gratitude to Stay Resilient

Life will throw challenges your way. **Gratitude is your shield.**

- Instead of saying, *"Why is this happening to me?"*, say *"What is this teaching me?"*
- Instead of thinking, *"I can't handle this,"*, say *"This is making me stronger."*
- Instead of focusing on what's missing, focus on what remains.

Gratitude doesn't ignore difficulty—it overcomes it.

How to Deepen Your Spiritual Connection Through Gratitude

Gratitude isn't just about thinking good thoughts. It's about practice. Here's how to integrate gratitude into your spiritual life:

1. Begin and End Your Day With Gratitude

- **In the morning,** thank God (or the universe) for another day of life.
- **At night,** reflect on the blessings of the day—even the small ones.

This simple habit grounds your mind in gratitude daily.

2. Express Gratitude in Prayer or Meditation

- **If you pray, start with gratitude.** Before asking for anything, acknowledge what you already have.
- **If you meditate, focus on gratitude.** Feel it in your body, in your breath, in your heart.

This shifts your entire spiritual practice.

3. Give to Others as an Act of Gratitude

Every major faith teaches that gratitude **isn't just about words—it's about giving.**

- Donate to charity.
- Help a friend in need.
- Serve your family and community.

The more you give, **the more you recognize how much you already have.**

Action Steps: Unleash the Power of Gratitude

1. Write down three things you're grateful for every morning.
2. Reframe one problem today—find something good in it.
3. Express gratitude to someone—send a message, make a call, or say it in person.
4. When a challenge hits, pause and ask: "What can I learn from this?"
5. End your day with gratitude—list one thing that went right, no matter how small.

Final Thought: Gratitude is the Force That Unlocks Everything

Your life will never be perfect—but gratitude makes it powerful.

- It turns struggles into strength.
- It turns opportunities into action.
- It turns ordinary days into extraordinary ones.

The most successful people aren't the luckiest or the smartest—they're the ones who have learned to see the good, act on it, and multiply it.

Gratitude is the secret ingredient to happiness, success, and resilience.

Start using it today—and watch how your life changes.

CHAPTER 8:

ACTION AND PERSISTENCE – THE TWIN FORCES OF SUCCESS

Core Principle: Ideas are worthless without action. Persistence turns action into achievement.

The world is filled with dreamers—people who have great ideas, big ambitions, and lofty goals. But the world rewards doers. The difference between those who succeed and those who don't isn't intelligence, talent, or luck. It's action.

And not just action, but relentless, focused, persistent action.

Earl Nightingale put it bluntly:

"Ideas are worthless unless we act on them."

You can read all the books, attend all the seminars, and make all the plans you want—but until you do something, nothing happens.

But action alone is not enough. Success doesn't come from just starting—it comes from sticking with it when the initial excitement fades, when obstacles appear, when things get hard.

The moment you combine decisive action with unwavering persistence, success becomes inevitable.

Why Most People Fail: The Curse of Inaction and Weak Persistence

Look around, and you'll see the same pattern everywhere: **people waiting.**

- Waiting for the perfect time.
- Waiting until they "feel ready."
- Waiting for conditions to be just right.

And while they wait, opportunities pass them by. The truth is, there is no perfect time. You will never feel completely ready. And conditions will never be perfect.

Successful people don't wait—they start.

But just as many people fail because they give up too soon. They take action, but at the first sign of difficulty, they quit.

They say things like:

- *"I tried, but it just didn't work out."*
- *"I gave it a shot, but it was too hard."*
- *"I wasn't seeing results fast enough."*

That's why persistence is the missing piece.

You don't plant a seed and expect a tree the next day. You keep watering it. You keep tending to it. You keep going.

Most people quit right before they were about to break through. They were digging for gold and stopped just inches from striking it.

Winners? They keep digging.

Persistence: The True Test of Success

Napoleon Hill devoted an entire chapter in *Think and Grow Rich* to **persistence**—because without it, nothing else matters.

He studied 500 of the wealthiest, most successful people of his time, and every single one had one thing in common:

They refused to quit.

Hill called persistence:

"The sustained effort necessary to induce faith."

And he was right. You don't just wake up believing in your success—you build that belief through daily action, daily progress, and daily commitment.

The greatest achievers in history weren't the ones who had the best start—they were the ones who refused to stop.

Real-World Examples of Action and Persistence in Motion

1. J.K. Rowling – From Rejection to Global Success

Before she became one of the most successful authors in history, J.K. Rowling was a struggling single mother, living on government assistance, battling depression, and facing rejection after rejection.

The idea for *Harry Potter* came to her in 1990 on a delayed train ride. She saw the story so vividly in her mind—a young boy who didn't yet know he was a wizard. But ideas mean nothing without action.

For the next five years, Rowling worked on the book while enduring some of the hardest moments of her life. Her mother died. Her marriage collapsed. She moved to Scotland, jobless, raising her infant daughter alone. At her lowest point, she described herself as being "as poor as it is possible to be in modern Britain, without being homeless."

But she kept writing. She wrote in cafes, pushing her baby's stroller back and forth to keep her asleep while she worked. She believed in the story, even when nobody else did.

Then came the rejection letters.

- Twelve different publishers rejected *Harry Potter and the Sorcerer's Stone*. Some told her it was too long, too complicated, or that kids wouldn't be interested.
- One agent suggested she get a day job because writing for a living wasn't realistic.
- She could have given up. She could have assumed they were right.

Instead, she persisted.

Finally, Bloomsbury took a chance on her—but only after the CEO's 8-year-old daughter read the manuscript and begged for more.

The result? Over 500 million copies sold. A billion-dollar empire. A global phenomenon.

Rowling's story proves one thing: Talent alone doesn't win. Persistence does. She kept going when everything told her to stop. And that's why she won.

2. Thomas Edison – Persistence Beyond the Lightbulb

Everyone knows the story of Thomas Edison's 10,000 failed experiments before he perfected the lightbulb. It's a powerful lesson in persistence, but what many don't realize is that the lightbulb wasn't his only battle.

Edison's greatest personal invention—the phonograph—was born out of the same relentless determination.

In 1877, Edison sketched out an idea for a device that could record and replay sound. No one had done it before. Scientists at the time didn't believe it was possible. The idea that sound could be captured and played back seemed like something out of fantasy.

But Edison didn't waste time debating whether it could be done—he got to work.

- He experimented with different materials—first using tin foil cylinders, then wax-coated discs.
- He faced failure after failure, as each prototype broke down or produced unintelligible sounds.
- He ignored the doubters, who told him sound recording had no future.

And then, after countless refinements, it worked. The phonograph became one of his greatest inventions—one that paved the way for the music industry, radio, and eventually, every audio recording device we use today.

Edison was asked how he kept going despite so many failed attempts. His response?

> **"Everything comes to him who hustles while he waits."**

That's persistence. Not just believing in an idea, but pushing forward every day—through every failure—until success is the only possible outcome.

That's the mindset of a winner. No quitting. No excuses. Just constant action and relentless persistence until the goal is reached.

3. Dwayne "The Rock" Johnson – From Rejection to Global Success

Before he became one of the highest-paid actors in Hollywood, Dwayne "The Rock" Johnson was just another guy who got cut from professional football.

At 22 years old, Johnson's dream was to play professional football. He trained relentlessly, earned a spot on the University of Miami's championship team, and set his sights on the NFL. But reality hit hard—he wasn't drafted. Instead, he signed with the Calgary Stampeders in the Canadian Football League. Two months later, he was cut.

He was broke. Had seven dollars in his pocket. Moved back in with his parents. The dream he had worked for his entire life? Gone.

Most people would have given up. Johnson didn't.

Instead of feeling sorry for himself, he pivoted. His father was a professional wrestler, and though Johnson had never planned to follow in his footsteps, he saw an opportunity.

- He started training harder than ever.
- He learned the business inside and out.
- He took every small opportunity, even when the pay was next to nothing.

His early wrestling career wasn't easy. Fans hated him at first—literally booed him out of arenas. But he refused to quit. He reinvented himself, developed his signature style, and became one of the greatest professional wrestlers of all time.

Then, just as he dominated wrestling, he reinvented himself again—this time as an actor. Hollywood executives doubted him. They told him to change his name, to lose weight, to be "more traditional." He refused. He stuck to who he was, put in the work, and eventually became the biggest box-office draw of his generation.

What's the lesson? Johnson's success didn't come from luck or talent alone—it came from taking action and refusing to quit. His persistence turned failure into fuel.

The Two Rules of Persistence: What to Do When You Want to Quit

Everyone wants to quit at some point. The difference between winners and losers is simple: winners keep going.

Here are the two rules to follow when you feel like giving up:

1. Follow the 24-Hour Rule

When you feel like quitting, **don't make a decision immediately.**

- Give yourself **24 hours** to clear your mind.
- Get some rest, step back, and come back with a fresh perspective.
- Most of the time, you'll realize quitting was just an emotional reaction.

Successful people feel like quitting too—but they don't let emotions dictate their future.

2. If You Must Quit, Quit the Plan—Not the Goal

Sometimes, the path you're on isn't working. That doesn't mean the goal is wrong—it just means you need to adjust your approach.

- If your business isn't growing, change the strategy—but don't abandon the vision.
- If a skill is hard to learn, adjust the method—but don't stop learning.
- If one attempt fails, make a new one—but don't give up.

The goal remains the same. The strategy evolves. Winners adapt—they don't quit.

Action Steps: How to Turn Relentless Action into a Habit

1. **Take immediate action on every idea.** Don't wait. Move now.
2. **Set a daily action target.** What must get done today to move forward?
3. **Develop a "no excuses" policy.** Either you do it, or you don't—no in-between.

4. **Follow the 24-hour rule before quitting anything.** Never make a quitting decision in frustration.
5. **Measure progress, not perfection.** Done is better than perfect.

Final Thought: The World Belongs to the Doers

Every success story starts with someone who took action and refused to quit.

The world isn't changed by people who talk about their ideas—it's changed by those who act on them.

If you remember nothing else from this chapter, remember this:

> You don't have to be the smartest. You don't have to be the most talented. You just have to be the one who refuses to stop.

Action and persistence are the two forces that separate the winners from everyone else.

If you commit to these two things, your success is inevitable.

CHAPTER 9:
THE NEW GOLD MINE – CREATIVITY AND INNOVATION

Core Principle: *The world belongs to those who think differently, create solutions, and take bold action.*

We are living in the most opportunity-rich era in history. Never before has it been so easy to create, to build, and to turn ideas into reality.

But here's the truth: opportunity is only visible to those who train themselves to see it.

Earl Nightingale put it simply:

> **"Creativity is simply looking at the same thing as everyone else but seeing something different."**

And that's the difference between those who innovate and those who get left behind.

Some people look at the world and see problems. Others see possibilities.

Some people wait for instructions. Others build the future.

Some people say, "That's how it's always been." Others ask, "How can it be better?"

Creativity and innovation are not luxuries. They are the new gold mine. The people who master them will shape industries, create wealth, and lead the future.

This chapter is about unlocking your creative mind, spotting opportunities before they're obvious, and turning ideas into action.

Why Most People Never Innovate

Most people believe creativity is something you're born with—that it's a special gift, reserved for artists, inventors, and so-called geniuses.

They're wrong.

Creativity is not a gift. It's a skill. And like any skill, it can be learned, trained, and strengthened.

So why do most people never develop it? Why do they live their entire lives following the crowd instead of leading it?

It comes down to three things: fear, conformity, and inaction.

1. Fear of Looking Foolish

The biggest killer of innovation isn't lack of intelligence—it's **fear.**

- Fear of failing.
- Fear of being wrong.
- Fear of what people will say.

This fear is so powerful that most people never share their ideas, never take a risk, never step out of line.

Look at any great innovator—Steve Jobs, Thomas Edison, Walt Disney. All of them were mocked, ridiculed, and doubted. If they had let fear stop them, the world would be very different today.

The difference? They didn't let fear control them. They understood a fundamental truth:

If people aren't laughing at your idea at first, it's probably not bold enough.

2. The Habit of Conformity

From an early age, we are trained to follow the rules.

- Schools teach kids to memorize answers instead of questioning them.
- Workplaces train employees to stick to the process, avoid risks, and blend in.

- Society rewards those who fit the mold—not those who break it.

And so, over time, people stop thinking for themselves. They assume the way things are is the way they must always be.

But innovation comes from the people who challenge the norm. Every breakthrough comes from someone who asked, "What if there's a better way?"

If you want to be an innovator, you must break free from the habit of conformity.

3. Lack of Action

The world is full of people with great ideas that never go anywhere.

Because ideas don't matter—execution does.

Most people say, *"I had that idea years ago!"* But when you ask what they did with it, the answer is always the same: nothing.

- They overthink.
- They analyze instead of act.
- They wait for the "perfect time."

But here's the truth: There is no perfect time.

If you wait for perfect conditions, you'll wait forever. The best innovators don't sit around hoping for the right moment—they start before they're ready.

The only way to test an idea is to act on it. You don't need permission. You just need to move.

The Choice is Yours

Every person has the ability to be creative. Every person has ideas that could change their life—or even the world.

But only a few will take action. Only a few will push past fear, break free from conformity, and execute.

Which one will you be?

The Power of Thinking Differently

The greatest breakthroughs don't come from people following the rules—they come from people breaking them.

The world doesn't reward those who play it safe. It rewards those who see what others don't, question the norm, and build something better.

Some of the biggest successes in modern history came from people who refused to accept things "as they are." They thought differently. They saw what was missing and created it.

Here's how three innovators—**Shigeru Miyamoto, Brian Chesky, and Zhang Yiming**—changed their industries by **thinking differently.**

Shigeru Miyamoto – Bringing Imagination to Gaming

In the late 1970s, video games were simple, repetitive, and forgettable. Most were just a few blocks bouncing across a screen. There was no storytelling, no emotional connection, no adventure.

Then came **Shigeru Miyamoto.**

Miyamoto didn't see video games as just entertainment. He saw them as a new form of storytelling, a way to create entire worlds.

- While other companies focused on arcade-style, high-score games, he created characters with personalities—heroes like Mario and Link.
- While others repeated the same formulas, he introduced gameplay that made players feel like they were on an actual adventure.
- His breakthrough game, Donkey Kong, was rejected at first—Nintendo's U.S. division thought it was too different. But he persisted, and the game became a massive hit.

Miyamoto's ability to think beyond what existed changed gaming forever. Today, franchises like Super Mario, The Legend of Zelda, and Pokémon exist because he dared to imagine something bigger.

Lesson? **Innovators don't accept limitations—they redefine what's possible.**

Brian Chesky – Turning a Couch Into a Billion-Dollar Business

In 2007, **Brian Chesky** and his roommate couldn't afford their rent. They had an idea: What if we rented out air mattresses in our apartment?

Sounds ridiculous, right? No one in their right mind would stay in a stranger's home.

At least, that's what everyone told them.

But Chesky saw an opportunity where others saw a dead end. Hotels were expensive. Travelers wanted affordable, local experiences. So instead of listening to the critics, he built Airbnb.

- Every investor laughed him out of the room. The idea seemed too risky, too strange.
- People said no one would trust strangers with their homes.

- The first version of Airbnb flopped—but instead of quitting, he and his co-founders sold cereal boxes to keep the company alive.

Today, Airbnb is worth over $70 billion.

Chesky didn't invent travel. He didn't invent renting homes. He just looked at both industries differently—and built a bridge between them.

Lesson? **Innovators don't listen to the doubters—they prove them wrong.**

Zhang Yiming – Reinventing How the World Consumes Content

When **Zhang Yiming** started ByteDance in 2012, search engines and social media platforms were already dominating the internet. Most people believed the digital landscape was set.

But Zhang saw something no one else did.

- While other platforms focused on who you follow, he built TikTok and Toutiao around what you engage with.
- Instead of relying on friends' recommendations, he used AI-driven algorithms to deliver the most engaging content instantly.

- While most companies thought short videos had no future, he saw them as the future of entertainment.

The result? TikTok became the fastest-growing social media platform in history.

What others saw as just another video app, Zhang turned into a global phenomenon.

Lesson? **Innovators don't accept the status quo—they rewrite the rules.**

The Takeaway: See What Others Don't

Every industry, every market, every business has gaps, inefficiencies, and untapped potential. The people who succeed are those who:

- **Look beyond what exists.**
- **Question why things are the way they are.**
- **Dare to create something different.**

The world doesn't need more of the same. It needs people willing to think differently, challenge the norm, and take bold action.

The question is—**will you be one of them?**

How to Train Yourself to Think Like an Innovator

Creativity isn't magic. It's a muscle. The more you train it, the stronger it gets. Here's how to develop it:

1. Ask "What if?" Every Day

- What if this process could be 10x faster?
- What if this product was easier to use?
- What if there's a simpler way?

Innovators challenge assumptions. They refuse to accept things "as they are."

2. Surround Yourself With Different Thinkers

If you only talk to people who think like you, you'll never think differently.

- Read books that challenge your perspective.
- Spend time with people outside your industry.
- Study different fields—science, psychology, history, art.

The best ideas often come from unexpected connections.

3. Take Action on Ideas Immediately

Ideas don't improve in your head. They improve through execution.

- If you have an idea, test it.
- If you see a problem, try to fix it.
- If you think of a better way, try it out.

The faster you act, the faster you learn.

4. Embrace Failure as Part of the Process

Every innovator fails—often.

- Edison failed thousands of times before perfecting his inventions.
- Melanie Perkins was rejected over 100 times before launching Canva.
- Musk's first SpaceX rockets exploded before he got it right.

Failure isn't the opposite of success. **It's part of it.**

Action Steps: How to Unlock Your Creative Power

1. **Write down 10 new ideas every morning.** Even if they're bad. The goal is to think.
2. **Look for problems in your industry.** Every problem is an opportunity for innovation.
3. **Ask "Why?" and "What if?" more often.** Question everything.
4. **Surround yourself with innovators.** Learn from those who think differently.

5. **Act fast.** Don't just think—test, build, experiment.

Final Thought: The Future Belongs to the Creators

The world rewards those who think differently, challenge assumptions, and take bold action.

If you train yourself to see opportunities, solve problems, and execute ideas, you will never be left behind.

If you remember one thing from this chapter, remember this:

> "Innovation isn't about waiting for permission. It's about creating something better—and making the world take notice."

The gold mine isn't in the ground. **It's in your mind.** Start digging.

CHAPTER 10:

THE 30-DAY EXPERIMENT – REINVENTING YOURSELF ONE MONTH AT A TIME

Core Principle: You can change your life in 30 days—if you commit to focused action.

The Power of the 30-Day Challenge – A Proven Path to Transformation

Most people believe change takes years. They assume success is a slow, painful climb that may never pay off.

They're wrong.

Earl Nightingale proved it over 70 years ago with his legendary 30-day challenge in *The Strangest Secret*. He didn't ask people to change their entire lives overnight. He didn't tell them success required years of struggle. He simply challenged them to take control of their thoughts and actions for 30 days—and see what happened.

And what happened? Those who truly committed saw undeniable transformations. Their thinking changed. Their habits improved. Their opportunities expanded.

Because success isn't about hoping for the future—it's about what you do every day.

Nightingale knew that if you focus on a single principle, apply it relentlessly for 30 days, and track your results, you will experience breakthroughs most people only dream about.

This isn't theory. It's a fact.

When you commit to a short, intense period of disciplined action, your results compound. One good decision leads to another. Small wins build momentum.

And by the time 30 days are over? You're a different person.

This chapter isn't about vague motivation. It's about proof. Proof that, in just one month, you can rewire your thinking, destroy old habits, and set yourself on a new course.

If you apply this correctly, you will achieve more in the next 30 days than most people do in a year.

This is your challenge. This is your moment.

Are you ready?

Why 30 Days? The Science Behind Short-Term Transformation

Why 30 days? Why not a week? Why not six months?

Earl Nightingale understood something decades ago that modern science now confirms: lasting change happens when action is repeated consistently over time—long enough to rewire habits, but short enough to maintain focus and intensity.

Thirty days is the perfect window for transformation. It's short enough to keep you engaged, yet long enough to break old patterns and build new ones.

Here's why it works—not just in theory, but in science, psychology, and real-world results.

1. The Habit Formation Process – Rewiring the Brain

Neuroscience tells us that habits are formed through a process called neuroplasticity. This means your brain is constantly changing, adapting, and forming new neural connections in response to repeated behaviors.

A study from University College London found that it takes between 21 and 66 days to form a new habit, with an average of about 30 days before a behavior starts becoming automatic.

- At first, your brain resists change. The old neural pathways—the ones built by your previous habits—try to keep you in place.
- But when you repeat a new behavior every single day, your brain lays down new wiring, making the habit easier and more natural over time.
- By the end of 30 days, the foundation is set. The new habit isn't just something you do—it's something you are.

By committing to a 30-day challenge, you aren't just "trying" a new habit—you're training your brain to make it permanent.

2. The Power of Focus – Eliminating Overwhelm

Most people fail at making changes because they try to do too much at once.

- They want to lose weight, start a business, save money, read more books, wake up early, and meditate—all at the same time.
- The result? They get overwhelmed and quit.

The 30-day challenge eliminates this problem by forcing you to focus on one major improvement at a time.

Science backs this up. Research shows that the brain struggles with multitasking. When you focus on too many things, your mental energy is divided, making it harder to build lasting change in any area.

But when you pour all your energy into one single habit for 30 days, your brain strengthens the neural circuits related to that habit, making it far more likely to stick.

> **"The successful person is the one who focuses on just one thing at a time and does it well."**
> – Earl Nightingale

3. The Commitment Effect – Using Psychology to Your Advantage

Studies in behavioral psychology prove that when people commit to short-term goals, they are far more likely to follow through.

Why? Because long-term goals feel vague and distant.

- Saying, *"I'll lose 30 pounds this year"* feels abstract.

- Saying, *"I will exercise for 30 minutes every day for the next 30 days"* feels immediate and achievable.

Short-term commitments eliminate mental resistance. The brain perceives them as manageable, making you more likely to follow through.

By committing to 30 days, you create a psychological contract with yourself—a clear, defined challenge that activates your motivation instead of overwhelming it.

4. Small Wins Create Big Momentum

Harvard Business School researchers discovered something powerful: small, daily progress is one of the biggest drivers of long-term success.

- When you complete a small challenge, your brain releases dopamine, a neurotransmitter linked to motivation and reward.
- This creates a positive feedback loop—you feel good about making progress, which makes you want to keep going.
- By stacking small wins every day for 30 days, you build unstoppable momentum.

This is why many people who commit to just 30 days of change find themselves continuing far beyond that—because success becomes addictive.

5. The Strangest Secret and the 30-Day Experiment

Earl Nightingale's original 30-day challenge wasn't just about habits—it was about proving to yourself that success is a mindset.

He asked his listeners to spend 30 days doing one thing: controlling their thoughts.

- Instead of focusing on fear, doubt, and obstacles, he challenged them to concentrate only on their goals.
- Instead of complaining about circumstances, he told them to act as if success was already on its way.
- Instead of waiting for "someday," he pushed them to live intentionally—starting immediately.

The results? Those who followed through experienced massive shifts in their careers, finances, and relationships—all in just 30 days.

Because when you take control of your mind, everything else follows.

The Verdict: 30 Days is the Fast Track to Transformation

Change doesn't have to take years. Science proves that when you focus on one goal for 30 days, track your progress, and build daily momentum, transformation happens faster than most people believe.

Earl Nightingale was right: **30 days of intense focus can accomplish more than years of scattered effort.**

Now the question is—**are you ready to commit?**

The Rules of the 30-Day Experiment

1. **Pick One Area of Focus** – Choose something specific: fitness, finances, mindset, business, or relationships.
2. **Take Daily Action** – No exceptions. **You must do something—every single day.**
3. **Track Progress** – Measure your results. Success isn't about effort—it's about outcomes.
4. **Eliminate Distractions** – Remove anything that slows you down. **For 30 days, you focus.**
5. **Adjust and Adapt** – If something isn't working, **modify the approach, not the goal.**

This isn't about vague self-improvement. It's about proving to yourself that massive change is possible in 30 days.

Real-World Examples of 30-Day Transformations

1. Matt D'Avella – The Minimalism Experiment

Matt D'Avella, a filmmaker, decided to declutter his life in 30 days.

- He eliminated 80% of his possessions.
- He tracked his spending and cut unnecessary expenses.
- He simplified his schedule, focusing only on what mattered.

By the end of 30 days, his life was lighter, clearer, and more focused. He didn't just clean his house—he rewired his mind.

2. Noah Kagan – The Fear Challenge

Noah Kagan, an entrepreneur, decided to eliminate fear in 30 days.

- He did one uncomfortable thing daily—asking for discounts, speaking in public, making cold calls.
- He learned that fear fades when you face it repeatedly.
- By the end of 30 days, his confidence had skyrocketed.

One month destroyed a lifetime of hesitation.

3. Tim Ferriss – Learning Any Skill in 30 Days

Tim Ferriss, best-selling author, believes you can master the basics of anything in 30 days.

- He used daily repetition and deliberate practice to learn languages, sports, and business strategies.
- He tracked progress aggressively, optimizing what worked and dropping what didn't.
- By the end of 30 days, he had acquired skills most people take years to develop.

If you dedicate 30 days to learning, you will be ahead of 99% of people.

How to Design Your Own 30-Day Experiment

Step 1: Choose One Focus Area

Don't try to change everything at once. **Pick one area** where you want rapid improvement:

- **Health** – Lose weight, build muscle, improve sleep.
- **Business** – Start a side hustle, increase sales, expand your network.

- **Mindset** – Overcome fear, build confidence, eliminate negativity.
- **Finances** – Save money, invest, pay off debt.

Success comes from **focusing on one thing intensely.**

Step 2: Define Your Daily Action

What will you do **every single day** to create results?

- **If it's fitness, you might work out daily for 30 minutes.**
- **If it's business, you might make five sales calls daily.**
- **If it's mindset, you might journal and meditate every morning.**

Action creates results. Without daily action, nothing changes.

Step 3: Track Your Progress

- **Keep a journal.** Write down what you did and how you feel.
- **Use a habit tracker.** Check off each successful day.
- **Measure improvement.** Progress isn't about how hard you work—it's about what you achieve.

Tracking keeps you accountable and motivated.

Step 4: Remove Distractions

For 30 days, **cut out anything that slows you down.**
- **Social media? Limit it.**
- **TV? Reduce it.**
- **Negative people? Distance yourself.**

For one month, **your goal is the only priority.**

Step 5: Evaluate and Adjust

Not everything will go perfectly. That's fine.
- If something isn't working, adjust the strategy.
- If you fall off track, get back on immediately.
- If you struggle, remind yourself: It's only 30 days. You can do anything for 30 days.

What Happens After 30 Days?

By the end of the experiment, one of two things will happen:

1. **You'll have results that prove what's possible.**
2. **You'll have built a habit that sticks.**

Either way, you win.

Most people never push themselves beyond their comfort zone. You will.

And once you see what's possible in 30 days, you'll never doubt yourself again.

Action Steps: Start Your 30-Day Experiment Today

1. Pick one area of life to transform.
2. Define one daily action you will take.
3. Commit for 30 days—no exceptions.
4. Track your progress.
5. Adjust and refine as needed.

The next 30 days will pass whether you take action or not. The question is:

> Will you stay the same, or will you reinvent yourself?

Final Thought: The Power of One Month

Most people wait their entire lives to change.

You don't have to.

If you fully commit to a 30-day challenge, your results will be undeniable.

> "In just one month, you can break old habits, build new ones, and prove to yourself that transformation is possible. The only thing stopping you is inaction. So start. Now."

Your future self is waiting. The countdown begins today.

CHAPTER 11:

WEALTH AND THE LAW OF MUTUAL EXCHANGE

Core Principle: Money is a byproduct of value. The more value you create, the more wealth you attract.

Earl Nightingale understood something most people never grasp:

Wealth isn't something you chase—it's something you attract by providing value.

The world doesn't reward effort alone. It rewards results. The more you contribute, solve problems, and improve the lives of others, the more money flows back to you.

This is the **Law of Mutual Exchange**—the timeless principle that states:

"You will be paid in direct proportion to the value you deliver to the marketplace."

If you understand this, you will never be broke another day in your life.

If you ignore it, you will struggle financially, no matter how hard you work.

This chapter is about unlocking wealth—not through get-rich-quick schemes or wishful thinking, but by applying the iron law of prosperity: Give more, serve better, and money will follow.

Why Most People Struggle Financially

Look around, and you'll see a painful truth: most people live paycheck to paycheck, constantly stressed about money.

Why? Because they misunderstand the true source of wealth.

- They think wealth comes from working harder.
- They think wealth is reserved for the lucky few.
- They think they need a high-paying job to be rich.

But hard work alone doesn't create wealth. If it did, construction workers and factory laborers would be millionaires.

Wealth comes from value, not effort.

And the people who create the most value in the world are the ones who attract the most money.

This explains why:

- A software engineer earns more than a fast-food worker—because they solve bigger, more complex problems.
- An entrepreneur can make millions while an employee stays stuck—because entrepreneurs create systems that serve thousands, while employees trade hours for dollars.
- A best-selling author earns more than an unknown writer—because they impact more people.

Money follows value. **Always.**

The Wealth Formula: How to Create Massive Value

Most people spend their lives chasing money—working harder, grinding longer hours, hoping for a raise or a lucky break.

That's the wrong approach.

Money isn't something you chase. It's something you attract by providing value.

If you want to create wealth, you need to stop asking, *"How can I make more money?"* and start asking, **"How can I create more value?"**

Because money is nothing more than a certificate of appreciation for value delivered.

Here's the formula—simple, unbreakable, and guaranteed to create wealth when applied.

1. Solve Bigger Problems

Wealth flows to those who solve problems.

The size of the problem you solve determines the size of your paycheck.

Think about it:

- A janitor cleans floors. A surgeon saves lives. Who makes more? The surgeon—because they solve a bigger problem.
- A local shop sells a few products. Amazon serves millions. Who makes more? Amazon—because they solve a global problem at scale.

Most people stay broke because they solve small problems.

If you want to increase your income, start solving bigger problems.

- A struggling entrepreneur asks, *"How can I make an extra $500 a month?"*
- A wealthy entrepreneur asks, *"How can I create a service that saves businesses thousands of dollars a year?"*

One is focused on small gains. The other is focused on massive value creation.

If you want to be rich, stop looking for money and start looking for problems to solve.

2. Serve More People

There's a reason why the wealthiest people in history are all entrepreneurs.

They understood a simple truth:

Money is a reflection of how many people you serve.

- A local bakery can only serve a few hundred customers. A national bakery chain serves millions.
- A personal trainer helps 10 people. An online fitness program helps 10,000.
- A freelancer trades time for money. An entrepreneur builds systems that make money while they sleep.

The lesson? **If you want to make more, you must serve more.**

Ask yourself:

- How can I reach **more** people?
- How can I scale my value beyond just **one-on-one interactions?**
- How can I leverage technology to **expand my impact?**

Your income is limited only by the number of people you help.

3. Increase Your Skills and Knowledge

You are paid for what you know and what you can do.

If you're not making the money you want, it's because your skills are not valuable enough in the marketplace.

- A doctor earns more than a cashier because their skills solve a more complex problem.
- A top salesperson earns more than a beginner because they understand persuasion and negotiation.
- A skilled investor makes money while they sleep because they know how to make money work for them.

If you want to earn more, you must become more.

- Read books.
- Take courses.
- Find mentors.
- Study successful people and copy what they do.

Your income is a reflection of your skillset. If you want to increase your earning power, increase your knowledge and expertise.

4. Build Wealth, Don't Just Earn Money

Most people focus on earning money. The wealthy focus on building assets.

- Employees trade time for money. When they stop working, the money stops.
- Entrepreneurs build systems. Even if they take a break, the money keeps flowing.

Think about this:

- J.K. Rowling wrote Harry Potter once—but earns royalties forever.
- Elon Musk built Tesla and SpaceX—his businesses generate billions even while he sleeps.

- Warren Buffett invested in companies decades ago—those investments still pay him today.

The goal isn't just to work harder. It's to build something that pays you repeatedly.

If you're only making money when you're working, you don't have true wealth—you just have a job.

The Bottom Line: Value First, Money Follows

The secret to wealth is not chasing money—it's creating value.

- Solve bigger problems.
- Serve more people.
- Improve your skills.
- Build assets that generate income.

Money isn't something you work for. It's something you earn by delivering value.

The bigger the value, the bigger the paycheck.

So ask yourself: How much value are you creating?

Real-World Examples of Wealth Creation

The world's wealthiest individuals didn't stumble upon their fortunes by accident. They **understood the Law of Mutual Exchange**—that wealth is created by solving problems, serving more people, and increasing value.

Here's how **Bernard Arnault, Jan Koum, and Masayoshi Son** applied these principles to build **billions in wealth** through smart thinking, bold action, and relentless value creation.

1. Bernard Arnault – Turning Luxury into an Empire

Bernard Arnault, the chairman and CEO of LVMH (Louis Vuitton Moët Hennessy), is one of the world's richest people — worth over $200 billion. But his fortune didn't come from a single business or invention. It came from understanding value and elevating it.

In the 1980s, Arnault saw something that others didn't: Luxury isn't just about products—it's about status, heritage, and exclusivity.

At the time, luxury brands were scattered, family-owned businesses. Arnault had a vision to bring them together under one powerhouse company.

- He acquired Dior, rescuing the struggling brand and turning it into a global icon.
- He bought Louis Vuitton, Moët & Chandon, and Hennessy, merging them into the world's most powerful luxury conglomerate.

- He expanded into fashion, jewelry, watches, and hospitality, transforming LVMH into a status symbol empire.

Arnault didn't just sell products—he sold identity, aspiration, and prestige. Today, LVMH dominates the luxury market, with over 75 brands and billions in annual revenue.

Lesson? Wealth follows those who understand perception, brand power, and premium value. Arnault didn't just sell goods—**he sold dreams.**

2. Jan Koum – From Food Stamps to Selling WhatsApp for $19 Billion

Jan Koum grew up dirt poor in Soviet-era Ukraine, moving to the U.S. as a teenager. His family survived on food stamps, barely making ends meet.

But Koum saw an opportunity: Communication should be simple, private, and accessible to everyone.

In 2009, he and a friend, Brian Acton, built WhatsApp—a messaging app designed to be free, fast, and encrypted. They rejected ads, pop-ups, and unnecessary features. Their goal? Let people talk freely, without distractions.

- WhatsApp spread like wildfire, reaching 400 million users in five years.

- They refused to sell out early, rejecting funding offers to keep their vision intact.
- In 2014, Facebook acquired WhatsApp for $19 billion—one of the largest tech deals in history.

Koum went from standing in welfare lines to becoming a billionaire—all because he solved a massive problem: simple, global communication.

Lesson? Wealth follows those who simplify complexity and remove friction. If you can make life easier for millions, **money will chase you.**

3. Masayoshi Son – Betting Big and Winning Bigger

Masayoshi Son, founder of SoftBank, is one of the most aggressive investors in history. He didn't build wealth by playing it safe—he built it by seeing the future before anyone else.

In the 1980s, he launched SoftBank, a tiny software distributor in Japan. But he had a bigger vision: Technology would shape the future.

- He invested early in Yahoo, making billions before the dot-com crash.
- He backed Alibaba with $20 million—an investment that turned into $60 billion.

- He launched the SoftBank Vision Fund, the largest tech investment fund in history, with $100 billion backing startups.

Son's biggest strength? Seeing potential before the world catches on. While others hesitated, he bet on the biggest tech revolutions before they exploded.

Today, SoftBank owns stakes in dozens of billion-dollar companies, from Uber to TikTok's parent company, ByteDance.

Lesson? Wealth follows those who see trends early and act boldly. The bigger the risk, **the bigger the reward.**

The Takeaway: Wealth Comes from Vision, Action, and Scale

Bernard Arnault, Jan Koum, and Masayoshi Son **built their fortunes by understanding value, solving problems, and scaling success.**

- Arnault mastered the psychology of luxury.
- Koum made communication simple and universal.
- Son saw the future of technology before anyone else.

They didn't just work hard—they thought differently, moved fast, and provided massive value.

The question is—**how will you do the same?**

Action Steps: How to Attract Wealth Starting Today

1. Identify a Problem to Solve

- What problems do people complain about?
- What skills do you have that can solve them?
- How can you provide a better solution?

2. Increase Your Value

- Learn high-income skills—sales, marketing, investing.
- Study wealthy people and copy their habits.
- Offer more value than you are paid for, and the money will follow.

3. Build Wealth Instead of Just Earning Money

- Start a side business.
- Invest in assets (stocks, real estate, or businesses).
- Stop trading time for money—**build something that pays you repeatedly.**

Final Thought: Money is a Reflection of Value

Most people chase money, but the wealthy create value and let money chase them.

If you increase your value to the world, your financial success is inevitable.

If you remember nothing else from this chapter, remember this:

> **"You will always be paid in direct proportion to the value you provide."**

The question is—**how much value will you create?**

CHAPTER 12:
A LIFE WORTH LIVING

Core Principle: *Success is not a destination. It is a way of life.*

Earl Nightingale often said that **success is the progressive realization of a worthy ideal.** That means success is not a finish line—it's the continuous journey of becoming more, doing more, and living with purpose.

A truly successful life isn't measured just by money or achievements. It's measured by impact, fulfillment, and the legacy you leave behind.

This final chapter is about what really matters—the kind of success that lasts beyond your lifetime.

If you live by the principles in this book, you won't just succeed. You will create a life worth remembering.

What Does It Mean to Live a Life Worth Living?

Most people drift through life, never stopping to ask if they're truly living or merely existing. They follow routines, chase distractions, and wake up years later wondering where their time went.

But a life worth living isn't about going through the motions. It's about living deliberately, growing daily, and leaving an impact that matters.

If you focus only on survival, life becomes a dull repetition of responsibilities. But when you pursue meaning, challenge yourself, and serve others, life takes on new energy.

Look at the greats—those who left an undeniable mark. They didn't live for comfort or security. They lived for something bigger than themselves.

- **Helen Keller** overcame blindness and deafness to inspire millions.
- **Leonardo da Vinci** never stopped learning, questioning, and creating.
- **Nelson Mandela** endured decades of hardship to fight for freedom.

None of them followed an easy path. But all of them lived lives worth remembering.

So ask yourself—what kind of life are you building? If it's not one filled with growth, purpose, and service, it's time to change course. Because in the end, the greatest tragedy isn't failure—it's looking back and realizing you never truly lived.

The Four Pillars of a Life Worth Living

A great life doesn't happen by accident. It's not about luck, wealth, or recognition. It's about who you become, how you grow, what you give, and what you leave behind.

Earl Nightingale taught that if you focus only on money or accolades, you may reach the top of the ladder only to find it was leaning against the wrong wall.

A life worth living is built on four unshakable pillars:

- **Purpose: Knowing Why You're Here**
- **Growth: Expanding Who You Are**
- **Contribution: Giving More Than You Take**
- **Legacy: Leaving Something That Outlasts You**

Master these, and you will live not just successfully—but meaningfully.

1. Purpose: Knowing Why You're Here

Most people wander through life without ever defining their purpose. They chase money, approval, or short-term pleasures, but none of it brings lasting fulfillment.

A life without purpose is like a ship without a rudder—it drifts wherever the wind blows, controlled by external forces.

But when you discover your purpose, everything changes. You wake up with energy. Your actions have meaning. Obstacles become challenges instead of roadblocks.

Purpose is your internal compass. It guides every decision, every effort, every goal.

Look at history's greatest achievers. They weren't just chasing wealth—they were driven by something bigger than themselves.

- **Mother Teresa** didn't dedicate her life to the poor for fame or money. She did it because she believed it was her calling.
- **Steve Jobs** didn't build Apple just to sell computers. He wanted to "put a dent in the universe."

- **Walt Disney** didn't create a billion-dollar empire for profit alone—he wanted to bring joy and imagination to the world.

Ask yourself: **What excites you? What would you do even if you weren't paid? What impact do you want to make?**

If you don't know the answer, start exploring. Try new things. Challenge yourself. Pay attention to what lights a fire inside you.

Because once you find your purpose, your life will never be the same.

2. Growth: Expanding Who You Are

A stagnant life is an unfulfilled life. If you're not growing, you're dying.

Every person who has achieved greatness has one thing in common: **they never stopped learning.**

- **Leonardo da Vinci** was a painter, scientist, engineer, and philosopher—because he never stopped asking questions.
- **Benjamin Franklin** mastered multiple disciplines, reinventing himself over and over again.
- **Sara Blakely** attributes her success to lifelong learning and relentless self-improvement.

Growth isn't just about skills or intelligence. It's about expanding your thinking, your character, and your vision.

- **Read every day.** Books are wisdom in written form—study them.
- **Challenge yourself.** Do something hard. Step outside your comfort zone.
- **Surround yourself with great minds.** You are the sum of the five people you spend the most time with—choose wisely.

The moment you stop growing is the moment you start declining.

So commit to daily improvement. Because the better you become, the greater your life will be.

3. Contribution: Giving More Than You Take

You don't take your money with you when you die. You don't take your trophies, your titles, or your possessions.

The only thing that lasts is what you did for others.

The happiest, most fulfilled people in the world are those who give. They understand that true success isn't about accumulation—it's about impact.

- **Andrew Carnegie** gave away over 90% of his wealth, funding libraries, universities, and research institutions.
- **Chuck Feeney**, a billionaire, quietly donated his entire fortune while he was still alive.
- **Malala Yousafzai** has dedicated her life to education, empowerment, and advocacy for girls worldwide. If your success benefits only you, **it's not real success.**

How are you serving others?

- **Mentor someone.** Teach what you've learned.
- **Donate time, resources, or skills.** Wealth isn't just about money—it's about value.
- **Help without expecting anything in return.** The more you give, the more life gives back to you.

True wealth is measured not by what you accumulate, but by what you contribute.

4. Legacy: Leaving Something That Outlasts You

At the end of your life, what will you leave behind?

A life worth living isn't just about what you do while you're here—it's about what continues long after you're gone.

- Earl Nightingale recorded *The Strangest Secret* in 1956. People still learn from it today.
- Thomas Edison died in 1931. His inventions still power our world.
- Maya Angelou's words still inspire millions, even though she's no longer here.

Your legacy isn't just about wealth or fame. It's about the impact you made, the people you helped, and the wisdom you left behind.

Ask yourself:

- What lessons do I want to pass on?
- What work do I want to be remembered for?
- How can I leave the world better than I found it?

You don't need to be famous to leave a legacy. **Every person you help, every life you touch, every contribution you make becomes part of your legacy.**

And in the end, that's all that matters.

Final Thought: Live with Intention

Most people drift through life without ever taking the wheel. They wait for the right time, the perfect opportunity, or some outside force to push them forward. But life doesn't wait for you to be ready.

Success is not an accident. Neither is happiness, fulfillment, or impact.

A great life is built on intentional action. It's about making deliberate choices—every single day—to become better, serve more, and leave something meaningful behind.

You now hold the blueprint. **The principles in this book are proven, timeless, and unbreakable.**

- **You become what you think about.** So guard your mind.
- **Goals give life direction.** Set them, pursue them relentlessly.
- **Success demands action and persistence.** Take the first step—and then another.
- **Service leads to prosperity.** Give more than you take.
- **Gratitude unlocks abundance.** Appreciate what you have while striving for more.
- **Growth never stops.** Read, learn, challenge yourself.
- **Your legacy is built today.** Make each day count.

Earl Nightingale taught us that you don't have to be perfect, and you don't have to have it all figured out. **You just have to start.**

Decide today—right now—to live with intention.

Because in the end, **the greatest tragedy isn't failure. It's never truly living at all.**

ABOUT THE AUTHOR

Vic Johnson was totally unknown in the personal development field in 2001. Since that time he's created some of the most popular personal development sites on the Internet. One of them, AsAManthinketh.net, has given away over 400,000 copies of James Allen's classic book.

A nine-time Amazon best-selling author, he's become an internationally known expert in goal achieving and hosted his own TV show, Goals 2 Go, on TSTN. He became a powerful authority in the self-publishing field and has taught thousands how to publish their first book. His three-day weekend seminar events, Claim Your Power Now, attracted such icons as Bob Proctor, Jim Rohn, Denis Waitley and many others.

This success has come despite the fact that he and his family were evicted from their home in 1996 and the next year his last automobile was repossessed. His story of redemption and victory has inspired subscribers from around the world as he has taught the powerful principles that created incredible wealth in his life and many others.

Two of his books, *Day by Day With James Allen* and *You Become What You Think About,* have become International best sellers and have been translated into Russian, Korean, Japanese, Czech, Slovak and Farsi.

OTHER BOOKS BY VIC JOHNSON

You Become What You Think About

Day by Day with James Allen

How To Write A Book This Weekend, Even If You Flunked English Like I Did

Goal Setting: 13 Secrets of World Class Achievers

It's Never Too Late And You're Never Too Old : 50 People Who Found Success After 50

52 Mondays: The One Year Path To Outrageous Success & Lifelong Happiness

The Magic of Believing: Believe in Yourself and The Universe Is Forced to Believe In You

Failure Is Never Final: How To Bounce Back Big From Any Defeat

Self Help Books: The 101 Best Personal Development Books

How I Created a Six Figure Income Giving Away a Dead Guy's Book

50 Lessons I Learned From The World's #1 Goal Achiever

How To Make Extra Money: 100 Perfect Businesses for Part-Time and Retirement Income

SYLVIA'S
FOUNDATION INC.

Sylvia Murphy Fanelli was born in the hills of Kentucky in 1906. At age 26 she married Victor Fanelli, the son of recent Italian immigrants. Several years later they moved to rural North Central Florida which was to be her home until she passed away in 1976. Ten years after their marriage Victor suffered an appendicitis attack and soon died of complications.

The 36-year-old Sylvia suddenly found herself a young widow with five children under the age of ten. Living in her adopted state of Florida, she faced her challenge without the aid of a nearby family and without significant governmental assistance. She had an eighth-grade education, no skills, she never owned an automobile (and never had a driver's license). Despite her obstacles, she managed to raise five children into responsible and productive citizens while modeling an incredibly positive attitude --- it is an attitude that still lingers today among those who were touched by her.

Sylvia's Foundation, Inc. is a non-denominational, not-for-profit organization that was chartered in Florida in September 2002 and has been recognized by the IRS as a tax-exempt organization that meets 501 (c)(3) requirements (this means your contributions are fully tax-deductible as allowed by law). It is named in honor of Sylvia Murphy Fanelli and is dedicated to serving today's "Sylvias" and their families.

Our mission is to develop programs that will improve the quality of life and make a difference for young, widowed moms and their children. These programs include educational aid and stipends and automobile and home ownership assistance grants.

Please see our website at **www.Sylvias-Love.org** or write us at:

Sylvia's Foundation Inc.
PO Box 1220
Melrose, FL 32666 USA

###